APPENDIX TO

CONTRACTS

UCC Article 2 (Sales)

Extracts from
Uniform Commercial Code (Articles 1 and 2), and
Revision of Uniform Commercial Code (Article 2 – Sales),
July 1997 Draft

Edited by

JOHN P. DAWSON
Late Charles Stebbins Fairchild Professor of Law
Harvard University

WILLIAM BURNETT HARVEY
Professor of Law and Political Science Emeritus
Boston University

STANLEY D. HENDERSON
F.D.G. Ribble Professor of Law
University of Virginia

NEW YORK, NEW YORK
FOUNDATION PRESS
1998

*TEXT IS PRINTED ON 10% POST
CONSUMER RECYCLED PAPER*

2nd Reprint — 2001

EDITORS' NOTE

The aim of this Appendix is to provide supporting materials for a first-year course in the law of Contracts. That body of rule and doctrine, historically and today, is largely a product of the decisions of "common law" courts. But statutes have increased in numbers and importance in the modern age. The most comprehensive statute bearing on the law of Contracts is Article 2 of the Uniform Commercial Code, which governs contracts for the sale of goods in forty-nine of our states (plus the District of Columbia and the Virgin Islands). The influence of Article 2, however, extends well beyond what it "governs" in a strict sense. As the study of Contracts reveals, Article 2 is used by lawyers, judges, and academics as a source of ideas and principles for analysis and resolution of disputes not involving goods at all. Perhaps the best evidence of the reach of UCC Article 2 is its overall impact on the writing of the Restatement (Second) of Contracts, an impact the second restaters themselves described as "profound."

We include here the provisions of Article 2 (Sales)—plus a few sections from Article 1 (General Provisions)—most likely to be of value in a first-year course in Contracts. For the Code sections of greatest importance in the study of rules applicable to both sales of goods and contracts generally, we have added the relevant parts of the section's Official Comment.

It is now necessary to add one thing more. In 1988, the Permanent Editorial Board for the Uniform Commercial Code, with the approval of the National Conference of Commissioners on Uniform State Laws and the American Law Institute, began a formal study of Article 2 in order to determine whether its text should be revised. The Study Group issued a Preliminary Report in 1990, recommending major revisions of Article 2. A Drafting Committee was then formed and the work begun in earnest, headed by Professor Richard E. Speidel of Northwestern as Reporter. As of this writing, the project, though still in draft form, is nearing completion; final approval of the Revision is expected in mid-1999.

We include here extracts from the most recent version of UCC Revised Article 2 (Sales), the July 1997 Draft. The sections are presented in text only, without the revisers' comments. Again, selections have been made on the basis of relevance to the introductory course in Contracts. There will no doubt be changes in the current draft as the revision project is concluded.

*

TABLE OF CONTENTS

*

APPENDIX TO

CONTRACTS

UCC Article 2 (Sales)

*

UNIFORM COMMERCIAL CODE *

EXTRACTS FROM ARTICLES 1 AND 2

1995 OFFICIAL TEXT

Table of Contents

Article 1

GENERAL PROVISIONS

Part 1

SHORT TITLE, CONSTRUCTION, APPLICATION AND SUBJECT MATTER OF THE ACT

Part 2

GENERAL DEFINITIONS AND PRINCIPLES OF INTERPRETATION

Article 2

SALES

Part 1

SHORT TITLE, GENERAL CONSTRUCTION AND SUBJECT MATTER

Part 2

FORM, FORMATION AND READJUSTMENT OF CONTRACT

Part 3

GENERAL OBLIGATION AND CONSTRUCTION OF CONTRACT

Part 5

PERFORMANCE

Part 6

BREACH, REPUDIATION AND EXCUSE

Part 7

REMEDIES

GENERAL COMMENT
of
NATIONAL CONFERENCE OF COMMISSIONERS ON UNIFORM STATE LAWS AND THE AMERICAN LAW INSTITUTE

This Comment covers the development of the Code prior to 1962. Its subsequent history leading to the 1962, 1966, 1972, 1977 and 1987 Official Text and Comment changes is contained in Reports and Forewords of the Permanent Editorial Board for the Uniform Commercial Code.

Uniformity throughout American jurisdictions is one of the main objectives of this Code; and that objective cannot be obtained without substantial uniformity of construction. To aid in uniform construction of this Comment and those which follow the text of each section set forth the purpose of various provisions of this Act to promote uniformity, to aid in viewing the Act as an integrated whole, and to safeguard against misconstruction.

This Act is a revision of the original Uniform Commercial Code promulgated in 1951 and enacted in Pennsylvania in 1953, effective July 1, 1954; and these Comments are a revision of the original comments, which were before the Pennsylvania legislature at the time of its adoption of the Code. Changes from the text enacted in Pennsylvania in 1953 are clearly legitimate legislative history, but without explanation such changes may be misleading, since frequently matters have been omitted as being implicit without statement and language has been changed or added solely for clarity. Accordingly, the changes from the original text were published, under the title "1956 Recommendations of the Editorial Board for the Uniform Commercial Code," early in 1957, with reasons, and revised Comments were then prepared to restate the statutory purpose in the light of the revision of text.

The subsequent history leading to the 1962 Official Text with Comments is set out in detail in Report No. 1 of the Permanent Editorial Board for the Uniform Commercial Code. . . .

Hitherto most commercial transactions have been regulated by a number of Uniform Laws prepared and promulgated by the National Conference of Commissioners on Uniform State Laws. These acts, with the dates of their promulgation by the Conference, are:

Uniform Negotiable Instruments Law 1896
Uniform Warehouse Receipts Act 1906
Uniform Sales Act 1906
Uniform Bills of Lading Act 1909
Uniform Stock Transfer Act 1909
Uniform Conditional Sales Act 1918
Uniform Trust Receipts Act 1933

Two of these acts were adopted in every American State and the remaining acts have had wide acceptance. Each of them has become a segment of the statutory law relating to commercial transactions. It has been recognized for some years that these acts needed substantial revision to keep them in step with modern commercial practices and to integrate each of them with the others.

The concept of the present Act is that "commercial transactions" is a single subject of the law, notwithstanding its many facets.

A single transaction may very well involve a contract for sale, followed by a sale, the giving of a check or draft for a part of the purchase price, and the acceptance of some form of security for the balance.

The check or draft may be negotiated and will ultimately pass through one or more banks for collection.

If the goods are shipped or stored the subject matter of the sale may be covered by a bill of lading or warehouse receipt or both.

Or it may be that the entire transaction was made pursuant to a letter of credit either domestic or foreign.

Obviously, every phase of commerce involved is but a part of one transaction, namely, the sale of and payment for goods.

If, instead of goods in the ordinary sense, the transaction involved stocks or bonds, some of the phases of the transaction would obviously be different. Others would be the same. In addition, there are certain additional formalities incident to the transfer of stocks and bonds from one owner to another.

This Act purports to deal with all the phases which may ordinarily arise in the handling of a commercial transaction, from start to finish.

Because of the close relationship of each phase of a complete transaction to every other phase, it is believed that each Article of this Act is cognate to the single broad subject "Commercial Transactions", and that this Act is valid under any constitutional provision requiring an act to deal with only one subject. See, for excellent discussions of the meaning of "single subject": House v. Creveling, 147 Tenn. 589, 250 S.W. 357 (1923) and Commonwealth v. Snyder, 279 Pa. 234, 123 A. 792 (1924).

The preparation of the Act (which Section 1–101 denominates the "Uniform Commercial Code") was begun as a joint project of The American Law Institute and the National Conference of Commissioners on Uniform

State Laws in 1942. Various drafts were considered by joint committees of both bodies and debated by the full membership of each organization at annual meetings.... The original drafting and editorial work which led to the 1952 edition of the Code was in charge of an Editorial Board of which United States Circuit Judge Herbert F. Goodrich of Philadelphia was Chairman.... The Chief Reporter of the Code was Professor Llewellyn, and the Associate Chief Reporter was Professor Soia Mentschikoff....

The actual drafting was done in some cases by practicing lawyers and in others by teachers of various law schools. The customary procedure required that before a draft was submitted for discussion to the general memberships of The American Law Institute and of the National Conference of Commissioners, it was successively approved by three groups.

The first group were the so-called "advisers", consisting of specially selected judges, practicing lawyers and law teachers. The advisers met with the draftsmen on frequent occasions to debate and iron out, not only the substance but the form and phraseology of the proposed draft.

After the draft was cleared by the advisers, it was meticulously examined by the next two groups—the Council of The American Law Institute and either the Commercial Acts Section or the Property Acts Section of the Conference of Commissioners.

When these bodies had given their approval to the draft, it came before the general membership both of the Institute and of the Conference for consideration.

In addition in the final stages leading to this 1962 edition each article was reviewed and discussed by a special Subcommittee for that article. Recommendations of the Subcommittee were reviewed and acted upon by the Enlarged Editorial Board, pursuant to authority from the sponsoring bodies.... After final approval of the Code by the Institute and the Conference, and in accordance with the practice of the Conference, the completed Code was submitted to the American Bar Association and was approved by the House of Delegates of that Association.

ARTICLE 1

GENERAL PROVISIONS

PART 1

SHORT TITLE, CONSTRUCTION, APPLICATION AND SUBJECT MATTER OF THE ACT

§ 1–101. Short Title.

This Act shall be known and may be cited as Uniform Commercial Code.

§ 1–102. Purposes; Rules of Construction; Variation by Agreement.

(1) This Act shall be liberally construed and applied to promote its underlying purposes and policies.

(2) Underlying purposes and policies of this Act are

    (a) to simplify, clarify and modernize the law governing commercial transactions;

    (b) to permit the continued expansion of commercial practices through custom, usage and agreement of the parties;

    (c) to make uniform the law among the various jurisdictions.

(3) The effect of provisions of this Act may be varied by agreement, except as otherwise provided in this Act and except that the obligations of good faith, diligence, reasonableness and care prescribed by this Act may not be disclaimed by agreement but the parties may by agreement determine the standards by which the performance of such obligations is to be measured if such standards are not manifestly unreasonable.

(4) The presence in certain provisions of this Act of the words "unless otherwise agreed" or words of similar import does not imply that the effect of other provisions may not be varied by agreement under subsection (3).

(5) In this Act unless the context otherwise requires

    (a) words in the singular number include the plural, and in the plural include the singular;

(b) words of the masculine gender include the feminine and the neuter, and when the sense so indicates words of the neuter gender may refer to any gender.

§ 1–103. Supplementary General Principles of Law Applicable.

Unless displaced by the particular provisions of this Act, the principles of law and equity, including the law merchant and the law relative to capacity to contract, principal and agent, estoppel, fraud, misrepresentation, duress, coercion, mistake, bankruptcy, or other validating or invalidating cause shall supplement its provisions.

§ 1–106. Remedies to Be Liberally Administered.

(1) The remedies provided by this Act shall be liberally administered to the end that the aggrieved party may be put in as good a position as if the other party had fully performed but neither consequential or special nor penal damages may be had except as specifically provided in this Act or by other rule of law.

(2) Any right or obligation declared by this Act is enforceable by action unless the provision declaring it specifies a different and limited effect.

Official Comment

1. First, ... the remedies in this Act are to be liberally administered to the end stated in the section. Second, ... compensatory damages are limited to compensation. They do not include consequential or special damages, or penal damages; and the Act elsewhere makes it clear that damages must be minimized. Cf. Sections 1–203, 2–706(1), and 2–712(2). The third purpose of subsection (1) is to reject any doctrine that damages must be calculable with mathematical accuracy. Compensatory damages are often at best approximate: they have to be proved with whatever definiteness and accuracy the facts permit, but no more. Cf. Section 2–204(3).

2. Under subsection (2) any right or obligation described in this Act is enforceable by court action, even though no remedy may be expressly provided, unless a particular provision specifies a different and limited effect. Whether specific performance or other equitable relief is available is determined not by this section but by specific provisions and by supplementary principles. Cf. Sections 1–103, 2–716.

3. "Consequential" or "special" damages and "penal" damages are not defined in terms in the Code, but are used in the sense given them by the leading cases on the subject.

§ 1–107. Waiver or Renunciation of Claim or Right After Breach.

Any claim or right arising out of an alleged breach can be discharged in whole or in part without consideration by a written waiver or renunciation signed and delivered by the aggrieved party.

Official Comment

This section makes consideration unnecessary to the effective renunciation or waiver of rights or claims arising out of an alleged breach of a commercial contract where such renunciation is in writing and signed and delivered by the aggrieved party. Its provisions, however, must be read in conjunction with the section imposing an obligation of good faith. (Section 1–203). There may, of course, also be an oral renunciation or waiver sustained by consideration but subject to Statute of Frauds provisions and to the section of Article 2 on Sales dealing with the modification of signed writings (Section 2–209). As is made express in the latter section this Act fully recognizes the effectiveness of waiver and estoppel.

PART 2

GENERAL DEFINITIONS AND PRINCIPLES OF INTERPRETATION

§ 1–201. General Definitions.

Subject to additional definitions contained in the subsequent Articles of this Act which are applicable to specific Articles or Parts thereof, and unless the context otherwise requires, in this Act:

(1) "Action" in the sense of a judicial proceeding includes recoupment, counterclaim, set-off, suit in equity and any other proceedings in which rights are determined.

(2) "Aggrieved party" means a party entitled to resort to a remedy.

(3) "Agreement" means the bargain of the parties in fact as found in their language or by implication from other circumstances including course of dealing or usage of trade or course of performance as provided in this Act (Sections 1–205 and 2–208). Whether an agreement has legal consequences is determined by the provisions of this Act, if applicable; otherwise by the law of contracts (Section 1–103). (Compare "Contract".) ...

(9) "Buyer in ordinary course of business" means a person who in good faith and without knowledge that the sale to him is in violation of the ownership rights or security interest of a third party in the goods buys in ordinary course from a person in the business of selling goods of that kind but does not include a pawnbroker. All persons who sell minerals or the like (including oil and gas) at wellhead or minehead shall be deemed to be persons in the business of selling goods of that kind. "Buying" may be for cash or by exchange of other property or on secured or unsecured credit and includes receiving goods or documents of title under a pre-existing contract for sale but does not include a transfer in bulk or as security for or in total or partial satisfaction of a money debt.

(10) "Conspicuous": A term or clause is conspicuous when it is so written that a reasonable person against whom it is to operate ought to have noticed it. A printed heading in capitals (as: NON-NEGOTIABLE BILL OF LADING) is conspicuous. Language in the body of a form is "conspicuous" if it is in larger or other contrasting type or color. But in a telegram any stated term is "conspicuous". Whether a term or clause is "conspicuous" or not is for decision by the court.

(11) "Contract" means the total legal obligation which results from the parties' agreement as affected by this Act and any other applicable rules of law. (Compare "Agreement".) . . .

(16) "Fault" means wrongful act, omission or breach.

(17) "Fungible" with respect to goods or securities means goods or securities of which any unit is, by nature or usage of trade, the equivalent of any other like unit. Goods which are not fungible shall be deemed fungible for the purposes of this Act to the extent that under a particular agreement or document unlike units are treated as equivalents. . . .

(19) "Good faith" means honesty in fact in the conduct or transaction concerned. . . .

(23) A person is "insolvent" who either has ceased to pay his debts in the ordinary course of business or cannot pay his debts as they become due or is insolvent within the meaning of the federal bankruptcy law. . . .

(25) A person has "notice" of a fact when

    (a) he has actual knowledge of it; or

    (b) he has received a notice or notification of it; or

    (c) from all the facts and circumstances known to him at the time in question he has reason to know that it exists.

A person "knows" or has "knowledge" of a fact when he has actual knowledge of it. "Discover" or "learn" or a word or phrase of similar import refers to knowledge rather than to reason to know. The time and circumstances under which a notice or notification may cease to be effective are not determined by this Act.

(26) A person "notifies" or "gives" a notice or notification to another by taking such steps as may be reasonably required to inform the other in ordinary course whether or not such other actually comes to know of it. A person "receives" a notice or notification when

    (a) it comes to his attention; or

    (b) it is duly delivered at the place of business through which the contract was made or at any other place held out by him as the place for receipt of such communications. . . .

(33) "Purchaser" means a person who takes by purchase.

(34) "Remedy" means any remedial right to which an aggrieved party is entitled with or without resort to a tribunal. . . .

(39) "Signed" includes any symbol executed or adopted by a party with present intention to authenticate a writing. . . .

(41) "Telegram" includes a message transmitted by radio, teletype, cable, any mechanical method of transmission, or the like.

(42) "Term" means that portion of an agreement which relates to a particular matter....

(46) "Written" or "writing" includes printing, typewriting or any other intentional reduction to tangible form.

§ 1–203. Obligation of Good Faith.

Every contract or duty within this Act imposes an obligation of good faith in its performance or enforcement.

Official Comment

This section sets forth a basic principle running throughout this Act. The principle involved is that in commercial transactions good faith is required in the performance and enforcement of all agreements or duties. Particular applications of this general principle appear in specific provisions of the Act such as ... the right to cure a defective delivery of goods (Section 2–508), the duty of a merchant buyer who has rejected goods to effect salvage operations (Section 2–603), substituted performance (Section 2–614), and failure of presupposed conditions (Section 2–615). The concept, however, is broader than any of these illustrations and applies generally, as stated in this section, to the performance or enforcement of every contract or duty within this Act. It is further implemented by Section 1–205 on course of dealing and usage of trade. This section does not support an independent cause of action for failure to perform or enforce in good faith. Rather, this section means that a failure to perform or enforce, in good faith, a specific duty or obligation under the contract, constitutes a breach of that contract or makes unavailable, under the particular circumstances, a remedial right or power. This distinction makes it clear that the doctrine of good faith merely directs a court towards interpreting contracts within the commercial context in which they are created, performed, and enforced, and does not create a separate duty of fairness and reasonableness which can be independently breached. See PEB Commentary No. 10, dated February 10, 1994.

It is to be noted that under the Sales Article definition of good faith (Section 2–103), contracts made by a merchant have incorporated in them the explicit standard not only of honesty in fact (Section 1–201), but also of observance by the merchant of reasonable commercial standards of fair dealing in the trade.

§ 1–204. Time; Reasonable Time; "Seasonably".

(1) Whenever this Act requires any action to be taken within a reasonable time, any time which is not manifestly unreasonable may be fixed by agreement.

(2) What is a reasonable time for taking any action depends on the nature, purpose and circumstances of such action.

(3) An action is taken "seasonably" when it is taken at or within the time agreed or if no time is agreed at or within a reasonable time.

§ 1–205. Course of Dealing and Usage of Trade.

(1) A course of dealing is a sequence of previous conduct between the parties to a particular transaction which is fairly to be regarded as establishing a common basis of understanding for interpreting their expressions and other conduct.

(2) A usage of trade is any practice or method of dealing having such regularity of observance in a place, vocation or trade as to justify an expectation that it will be observed with respect to the transaction in question. The existence and scope of such a usage are to be proved as facts. If it is established that such a usage is embodied in a written trade code or similar writing the interpretation of the writing is for the court.

(3) A course of dealing between parties and any usage of trade in the vocation or trade in which they are engaged or of which they are or should be aware give particular meaning to and supplement or qualify terms of an agreement.

(4) The express terms of an agreement and an applicable course of dealing or usage of trade shall be construed wherever reasonable as consistent with each other; but when such construction is unreasonable express terms control both course of dealing and usage of trade and course of dealing controls usage of trade.

(5) An applicable usage of trade in the place where any part of performance is to occur shall be used in interpreting the agreement as to that part of the performance.

(6) Evidence of a relevant usage of trade offered by one party is not admissible unless and until he has given the other party such notice as the court finds sufficient to prevent unfair surprise to the latter.

Official Comment

1. This Act rejects both the "lay-dictionary" and the "conveyancer's" reading of a commercial agreement. Instead the meaning of the agreement of the parties is to be determined by the language used by them and by their action, read and interpreted in the light of commercial practices and other surrounding circumstances. The measure and background for interpretation are set by the commercial context, which may explain and supplement even the language of a formal or final writing....

3. "Course of dealing" may enter the agreement either by explicit provisions of the agreement or by tacit recognition.

4. This Act deals with "usage of trade" as a factor in reaching the commercial meaning of the agreement which the parties have made. The language used is to be interpreted as meaning what it may fairly be expected to mean to parties involved in the particular commercial transaction in a given locality or in a given vocation or trade. By adopting in this context the term "usage of trade" this Act expresses its intent to reject those cases which see evidence of "custom" as representing an effort to displace or negate "established rules of law". A distinction is to be drawn between mandatory rules of law such as the Statute of Frauds provisions of Article

2 on Sales whose very office is to control and restrict the actions of the parties, and which cannot be abrogated by agreement, or by a usage of trade, and those rules of law (such as those in Part 3 of Article 2 on Sales) which fill in points which the parties have not considered and in fact agreed upon. The latter rules hold "unless otherwise agreed" but yield to the contrary agreement of the parties. Part of the agreement of the parties to which such rules yield is to be sought for in the usages of trade which furnish the background and give particu- lar meaning to the language used, and are the framework of common under- standing controlling any general rules of law which hold only when there is no such understanding. . . .

8. Although the terms in which this Act defines "agreement" include the elements of course of dealing and usage of trade, the fact that express reference is made in some sections to those elements is not to be construed as carrying a contrary intent or impli- cation elsewhere. Compare Section 1–102(4). . . .

§ 1–206. Statute of Frauds for Kinds of Personal Property Not Otherwise Covered.

(1) Except in the cases described in subsection (2) of this section a contract for the sale of personal property is not enforceable by way of action or defense beyond five thousand dollars in amount or value of remedy unless there is some writing which indicates that a contract for sale has been made between the parties at a defined or stated price, reasonably identifies the subject matter, and is signed by the party against whom enforcement is sought or by his authorized agent.

(2) Subsection (1) of this section does not apply to contracts for the sale of goods (Section 2–201) nor of securities (Section 8–113) nor to security agreements (Section 9–203).

§ 1–207. Performance or Acceptance Under Reservation of Rights.

(1) A party who with explicit reservation of rights performs or prom- ises performance or assents to performance in a manner demanded or offered by the other party does not thereby prejudice the rights reserved. Such words as "without prejudice", "under protest" or the like are sufficient.

(2) Subsection (1) does not apply to an accord and satisfaction.

As amended in 1990.

Official Comment

1. This section provides ma- chinery for the continuation of per- formance along the lines contemplat- ed by the contract despite a pending dispute, by adopting the mercantile device of going ahead with delivery, acceptance, or payment "without prejudice," "under protest," "under reserve," "with reservation of all our rights," and the like. All of these phrases completely reserve all rights within the meaning of this sec- tion. . . .

2.   This section does not add any new requirement of language of reservation where not already required by law, but merely provides a specific measure on which a party can rely as he makes or concurs in any interim adjustment in the course of performance. It does not affect or impair the provisions of this Act such as those under which the buyer's remedies for defect survive acceptance without being expressly claimed if notice of the defects is given within a reasonable time. Nor does it disturb the policy of those cases which restrict the effect of a waiver of a defect to reasonable limits under the circumstances, even though no such reservation is expressed.

The section is not addressed to the creation or loss of remedies in the ordinary course of performance but rather to a method of procedure where one party is claiming as of right something which the other feels to be unwarranted.

3.   Judicial authority was divided on the issue of whether former Section 1–207 (present subsection (1)) applied to an accord and satisfaction. Typically the cases involved attempts to reach an accord and satisfaction by use of a check tendered in full satisfaction of a claim. Subsection (2) of revised Section 1–207 resolves this conflict by stating that Section 1–207 does not apply to an accord and satisfaction. Section 3–311 of revised Article 3 governs if an accord and satisfaction is attempted by tender of a negotiable instrument as stated in that section. If Section 3–311 does not apply, the issue of whether an accord and satisfaction has been effected is determined by the law of contract. Whether or not Section 3–311 applies, Section 1–207 has no application to an accord and satisfaction.

ARTICLE 2

SALES

PART 1

SHORT TITLE, GENERAL CONSTRUCTION AND SUBJECT MATTER

§ 2-101. Short Title.

This Article shall be known and may be cited as Uniform Commercial Code—Sales.

§ 2-102. Scope; Certain Security and Other Transactions Excluded From This Article.

Unless the context otherwise requires, this Article applies to transactions in goods; it does not apply to any transaction which although in the form of an unconditional contract to sell or present sale is intended to operate only as a security transaction nor does this Article impair or repeal any statute regulating sales to consumers, farmers or other specified classes of buyers.

§ 2-103. Definitions....

(1) In this Article unless the context otherwise requires

(a) "Buyer" means a person who buys or contracts to buy goods.

(b) "Good faith" in the case of a merchant means honesty in fact and the observance of reasonable commercial standards of fair dealing in the trade.

(c) "Receipt" of goods means taking physical possession of them.

(d) "Seller" means a person who sells or contracts to sell goods....

§ 2-104. Definitions: "Merchant"; "Between Merchants"....

(1) "Merchant" means a person who deals in goods of the kind or otherwise by his occupation holds himself out as having knowledge or skill peculiar to the practices or goods involved in the transaction or to whom

such knowledge or skill may be attributed by his employment of an agent or broker or other intermediary who by his occupation holds himself out as having such knowledge or skill . . . .

(3) "Between merchants" means in any transaction with respect to which both parties are chargeable with the knowledge or skill of merchants.

Official Comment

1. This Article assumes that transactions between professionals in a given field require special and clear rules which may not apply to a casual or inexperienced seller or buyer. It thus adopts a policy of expressly stating rules applicable "between merchants" and "as against a merchant", wherever they are needed instead of making them depend upon the circumstances of each case as in the statutes cited above. This section lays the foundation of this policy by defining those who are to be regarded as professionals or "merchants" and by stating when a transaction is deemed to be "between merchants".

2. The term "merchant" as defined here roots in the "law merchant" concept of a professional in business. The professional status under the definition may be based upon specialized knowledge as to the goods, specialized knowledge as to business practices, or specialized knowledge as to both and which kind of specialized knowledge may be sufficient to establish the merchant status is indicated by the nature of the provisions . . . .

§ 2–105. Definitions: Transferability; "Goods"; "Future" Goods; "Lot"; "Commercial Unit".

(1) "Goods" means all things (including specially manufactured goods) which are movable at the time of identification to the contract for sale other than the money in which the price is to be paid, investment securities (Article 8) and things in action. "Goods" also includes the unborn young of animals and growing crops and other identified things attached to realty as described in the section on goods to be severed from realty (Section 2–107).

(2) Goods must be both existing and identified before any interest in them can pass. Goods which are not both existing and identified are "future" goods. A purported present sale of future goods or of any interest therein operates as a contract to sell . . . .

(5) "Lot" means a parcel or a single article which is the subject matter of a separate sale or delivery, whether or not it is sufficient to perform the contract.

(6) "Commercial unit" means such a unit of goods as by commercial usage is a single whole for purposes of sale and division of which materially impairs its character or value on the market or in use. A commercial unit may be a single article (as a machine) or a set of articles (as a suite of furniture or an assortment of sizes) or a quantity (as a bale, gross, or carload) or any other unit treated in use or in the relevant market as a single whole.

§ 2–106. Definitions: "Contract"; "Agreement"; "Contract for Sale"; "Sale"; "Present Sale"; "Conforming" to Contract; "Termination"; "Cancellation".

(1) In this Article unless the context otherwise requires "contract" and "agreement" are limited to those relating to the present or future sale of goods. "Contract for sale" includes both a present sale of goods and a contract to sell goods at a future time. A "sale" consists in the passing of title from the seller to the buyer for a price (Section 2–401). A "present sale" means a sale which is accomplished by the making of the contract.

(2) Goods or conduct including any part of a performance are "conforming" or conform to the contract when they are in accordance with the obligations under the contract.

(3) "Termination" occurs when either party pursuant to a power created by agreement or law puts an end to the contract otherwise than for its breach. On "termination" all obligations which are still executory on both sides are discharged but any right based on prior breach or performance survives.

(4) "Cancellation" occurs when either party puts an end to the contract for breach by the other and its effect is the same as that of "termination" except that the cancelling party also retains any remedy for breach of the whole contract or any unperformed balance.

§ 2–107. Goods to Be Severed From Realty: Recording.

(1) A contract for the sale of minerals or the like (including oil and gas) or a structure or its materials to be removed from realty is a contract for the sale of goods within this Article if they are to be severed by the seller but until severance a purported present sale thereof which is not effective as a transfer of an interest in land is effective only as a contract to sell.

(2) A contract for the sale apart from the land of growing crops or other things attached to realty and capable of severance without material harm thereto but not described in subsection (1) or of timber to be cut is a contract for the sale of goods within this Article whether the subject matter is to be severed by the buyer or by the seller even though it forms part of the realty at the time of contracting, and the parties can by identification effect a present sale before severance.

(3) The provisions of this section are subject to any third party rights provided by the law relating to realty records, and the contract for sale may be executed and recorded as a document transferring an interest in land and shall then constitute notice to third parties of the buyer's rights under the contract for sale.

As amended in 1972.

PART 2

FORM, FORMATION AND READJUSTMENT OF CONTRACT

§ 2–201. Formal Requirements; Statute of Frauds.

(1) Except as otherwise provided in this section a contract for the sale of goods for the price of $500 or more is not enforceable by way of action or defense unless there is some writing sufficient to indicate that a contract for sale has been made between the parties and signed by the party against whom enforcement is sought or by his authorized agent or broker. A writing is not insufficient because it omits or incorrectly states a term agreed upon but the contract is not enforceable under this paragraph beyond the quantity of goods shown in such writing.

(2) Between merchants if within a reasonable time a writing in confirmation of the contract and sufficient against the sender is received and the party receiving it has reason to know its contents, it satisfies the requirements of subsection (1) against such party unless written notice of objection to its contents is given within 10 days after it is received.

(3) A contract which does not satisfy the requirements of subsection (1) but which is valid in other respects is enforceable

(a) if the goods are to be specially manufactured for the buyer and are not suitable for sale to others in the ordinary course of the seller's business and the seller, before notice of repudiation is received and under circumstances which reasonably indicate that the goods are for the buyer, has made either a substantial beginning of their manufacture or commitments for their procurement; or

(b) if the party against whom enforcement is sought admits in his pleading, testimony or otherwise in court that a contract for sale was made, but the contract is not enforceable under this provision beyond the quantity of goods admitted; or

(c) with respect to goods for which payment has been made and accepted or which have been received and accepted (Sec. 2–606).

Official Comment

1. The required writing need not contain all the material terms of the contract and such material terms as are stated need not be precisely stated. All that is required is that the writing afford a basis for believing that the offered oral evidence rests on a real transaction. It may be written in lead pencil on a scratch pad. It need not indicate which party is the buyer and which the seller. The only term which must appear is the quanti-

ty term which need not be accurately stated but recovery is limited to the amount stated. The price, time and place of payment or delivery, the general quality of the goods, or any particular warranties may all be omitted.

Special emphasis must be placed on the permissibility of omitting the price term in view of the insistence of some courts on the express inclusion of this term even where the parties have contracted on the basis of a published price list. . . . [I]f the price is not stated in the memorandum it can normally be supplied without danger of fraud. Of course if the "price" consists of goods rather than money the quantity of goods must be stated.

Only three definite and invariable requirements as to the memorandum are made by this subsection. First, it must evidence a contract for the sale of goods; second, it must be "signed", a word which includes any authentication which identifies the party to be charged; and third, it must specify a quantity.

2. "Partial performance" as a substitute for the required memorandum can validate the contract only for the goods which have been accepted or for which payment has been made and accepted.

Receipt and acceptance either of goods or of the price constitutes an unambiguous overt admission by both parties that a contract actually exists. If the court can make a just apportionment, therefore, the agreed price of any goods actually delivered can be recovered without a writing or, if the price has been paid, the seller can be forced to deliver an apportionable part of the goods. The overt actions of the parties make admissible evidence of the other terms of the contract necessary to a just apportionment. . . .

Part performance by the buyer requires the delivery of something by him that is accepted by the seller as such performance. Thus, part payment may be made by money or check, accepted by the seller. If the agreed price consists of goods or services, then they must also have been delivered and accepted.

3. Between merchants, failure to answer a written confirmation of a contract within ten days of receipt is tantamount to a writing under subsection (2) and is sufficient against both parties under subsection (1). The only effect, however, is to take away from the party who fails to answer the defense of the Statute of Frauds; the burden of persuading the trier of fact that a contract was in fact made orally prior to the written confirmation is unaffected. Compare the effect of a failure to reply under Section 2–207. . . .

6. It is not necessary that the writing be delivered to anybody. It need not be signed or authenticated by both parties but it is, of course, not sufficient against one who has not signed it. . . .

7. If the making of a contract is admitted in court, either in a written pleading, by stipulation or by oral statement before the court, no additional writing is necessary for protection against fraud. Under this section it is no longer possible to admit the contract in court and still treat the Statute as a defense. However, the contract is not thus conclusively established. The admission so made by a party is itself evidential against him of the truth of the facts so admitted and of nothing more; as against the other party, it is not evidential at all.

§ 2–202. Final Written Expression: Parol or Extrinsic Evidence.

Terms with respect to which the confirmatory memoranda of the parties agree or which are otherwise set forth in a writing intended by the parties as a final expression of their agreement with respect to such terms as are included therein may not be contradicted by evidence of any prior agreement or of a contemporaneous oral agreement but may be explained or supplemented

(a) by course of dealing or usage of trade (Section 1–205) or by course of performance (Section 2–208); and

(b) by evidence of consistent additional terms unless the court finds the writing to have been intended also as a complete and exclusive statement of the terms of the agreement.

Official Comment

1. This section definitely rejects:

(a) Any assumption that because a writing has been worked out which is final on some matters, it is to be taken as including all the matters agreed upon;

(b) The premise that the language used has the meaning attributable to such language by rules of construction existing in the law rather than the meaning which arises out of the commercial context in which it is used; and

(c) The requirement that a condition precedent to the admissibility of the type of evidence specified in paragraph (a) is an original determination by the court that the language used is ambiguous.

2. Paragraph (a) makes admissible evidence of course of dealing, usage of trade and course of performance to explain or supplement the terms of any writing stating the agreement of the parties in order that the true understanding of the parties as to the agreement may be reached. Such writings are to be read on the assumption that the course of prior dealings between the parties and the usages of trade were taken for granted when the document was phrased. Unless carefully negated they have become an element of the meaning of the words used. Similarly, the course of actual performance by the parties is considered the best indication of what they intended the writing to mean.

3. Under paragraph (b) consistent additional terms, not reduced to writing, may be proved unless the court finds that the writing was intended by both parties as a complete and exclusive statement of all the terms. If the additional terms are such that, if agreed upon, they would certainly have been included in the document in the view of the court, then evidence of their alleged making must be kept from the trier of fact.

§ 2–203. Seals Inoperative.

The affixing of a seal to a writing evidencing a contract for sale or an offer to buy or sell goods does not constitute the writing a sealed instrument and the law with respect to sealed instruments does not apply to such a contract or offer.

§ 2–204. Formation in General.

(1) A contract for sale of goods may be made in any manner sufficient to show agreement, including conduct by both parties which recognizes the existence of such a contract.

(2) An agreement sufficient to constitute a contract for sale may be found even though the moment of its making is undetermined.

(3) Even though one or more terms are left open a contract for sale does not fail for indefiniteness if the parties have intended to make a contract and there is a reasonably certain basis for giving an appropriate remedy.

Official Comment

Subsection (1) continues without change the basic policy of recognizing any manner of expression of agreement, oral, written or otherwise. The legal effect of such an agreement is, of course, qualified by other provisions of this Article.

Under subsection (1) appropriate conduct by the parties may be sufficient to establish an agreement. Subsection (2) is directed primarily to the situation where the interchanged correspondence does not disclose the exact point at which the deal was closed, but the actions of the parties indicate that a binding obligation has been undertaken.

Subsection (3) states the principle as to "open terms" underlying later sections of the Article. If the parties intend to enter into a binding agreement, this subsection recognizes that agreement as valid in law, despite missing terms, if there is any reasonably certain basis for granting a remedy. The test is not certainty as to what the parties were to do nor as to the exact amount of damages due the plaintiff. Nor is the fact that one or more terms are left to be agreed upon enough of itself to defeat an otherwise adequate agreement. Rather, commercial standards on the point of "indefiniteness" are intended to be applied, this Act making provision elsewhere for missing terms needed for performance, open price, remedies and the like.

The more terms the parties leave open, the less likely it is that they have intended to conclude a binding agreement, but their actions may be frequently conclusive on the matter despite the omissions.

§ 2–205. Firm Offers.

An offer by a merchant to buy or sell goods in a signed writing which by its terms gives assurance that it will be held open is not revocable, for lack of consideration, during the time stated or if no time is stated for a reasonable time, but in no event may such period of irrevocability exceed three months; but any such term of assurance on a form supplied by the offeree must be separately signed by the offeror.

Official Comment

. . .

2. The primary purpose of this section is to give effect to the deliberate intention of a merchant to make a current firm offer binding. The deliberation is shown in the case of an individualized document by the merchant's signature to the offer, and in the case of an offer included on a form supplied by the other party to the

transaction by the separate signing of the particular clause which contains the offer. "Signed" here also includes authentication but the reasonableness of the authentication herein allowed must be determined in the light of the purpose of the section. The circumstances surrounding the signing may justify something less than a formal signature or initialing but typically the kind of authentication involved here would consist of a minimum of initialing of the clause involved. A handwritten memorandum on the writer's letterhead purporting in its terms to "confirm" a firm offer already made would be enough to satisfy this section, although not subscribed, since under the circumstances it could not be considered a memorandum of mere negotiation and it would adequately show its own authenticity. Similarly, an authorized telegram will suffice, and this is true even though the original draft contained only a typewritten signature. However, despite settled courses of dealing or usages of the trade whereby firm offers are made by oral communication and relied upon without more evidence, such offers remain revocable under this Article since authentication by a writing is the essence of this section.

3. This section is intended to apply to current "firm" offers and not to long term options, and an outside time limit of three months during which such offers remain irrevocable has been set.... A promise made for a longer period will operate under this section to bind the offeror only for the first three months of the period but may of course be renewed. If supported by consideration it may continue for as long as the parties specify. This section deals only with the offer which is not supported by consideration....

§ 2–206. Offer and Acceptance in Formation of Contract.

(1) Unless otherwise unambiguously indicated by the language or circumstances

(a) an offer to make a contract shall be construed as inviting acceptance in any manner and by any medium reasonable in the circumstances;

(b) an order or other offer to buy goods for prompt or current shipment shall be construed as inviting acceptance either by a prompt promise to ship or by the prompt or current shipment of conforming or non-conforming goods, but such a shipment of non-conforming goods does not constitute an acceptance if the seller seasonably notifies the buyer that the shipment is offered only as an accommodation to the buyer.

(2) Where the beginning of a requested performance is a reasonable mode of acceptance an offeror who is not notified of acceptance within a reasonable time may treat the offer as having lapsed before acceptance.

Official Comment

1. Any reasonable manner of acceptance is intended to be regarded as available unless the offeror has made quite clear that it will not be acceptable. Former technical rules as to acceptance, such as requiring that telegraphic offers be accepted by telegraphed acceptance, etc., are rejected

and a criterion that the acceptance be "in any manner and by any medium reasonable under the circumstances," is substituted. This section is intended to remain flexible and its applicability to be enlarged as new media of communication develop or as the more time-saving present day media come into general use.

2. Either shipment or a prompt promise to ship is made a proper means of acceptance of an offer looking to current shipment. In accordance with ordinary commercial understanding the section interprets an order looking to current shipment as allowing acceptance either by actual shipment or by a prompt promise to ship and rejects the artificial theory that only a single mode of acceptance is normally envisaged by an offer. This is true even though the language of the offer happens to be "ship at once" or the like....

3. The beginning of performance by an offeree can be effective as acceptance so as to bind the offeror only if followed within a reasonable time by notice to the offeror. Such a beginning of performance must unambiguously express the offeree's intention to engage himself. For the protection of both parties it is essential that notice follow in due course to constitute acceptance. Nothing in this section however bars the possibility that under the common law performance begun may have an intermediate effect of temporarily barring revocation of the offer, or at the offeror's option, final effect in constituting acceptance.

4. Subsection (1)(b) deals with the situation where a shipment made following an order is shown by a notification of shipment to be referable to that order but has a defect. Such a non-conforming shipment is normally to be understood as intended to close the bargain, even though it proves to have been at the same time a breach. However, the seller by stating that the shipment is non-conforming and is offered only as an accommodation to the buyer keeps the shipment or notification from operating as an acceptance.

§ 2–207. Additional Terms in Acceptance or Confirmation.

(1) A definite and seasonable expression of acceptance or a written confirmation which is sent within a reasonable time operates as an acceptance even though it states terms additional to or different from those offered or agreed upon, unless acceptance is expressly made conditional on assent to the additional or different terms.

(2) The additional terms are to be construed as proposals for addition to the contract. Between merchants such terms become part of the contract unless:

(a) the offer expressly limits acceptance to the terms of the offer;

(b) they materially alter it; or

(c) notification of objection to them has already been given or is given within a reasonable time after notice of them is received.

(3) Conduct by both parties which recognizes the existence of a contract is sufficient to establish a contract for sale although the writings of the parties do not otherwise establish a contract. In such case the terms of the particular contract consist of those terms on which the writings of the parties agree, together with any supplementary terms incorporated under any other provisions of this Act.

Official Comment

1. This section is intended to deal with two typical situations. The one is the written confirmation, where an agreement has been reached either orally or by informal correspondence between the parties and is followed by one or both of the parties sending formal memoranda embodying the terms so far as agreed upon and adding terms not discussed. The other situation is offer and acceptance, in which a wire or letter expressed and intended as an acceptance or the closing of an agreement adds further minor suggestions or proposals such as "ship by Tuesday," "rush," "ship draft against bill of lading inspection allowed," or the like. A frequent example of the second situation is the exchange of printed purchase order and acceptance (sometimes called "acknowledgment") forms. Because the forms are oriented to the thinking of the respective drafting parties, the terms contained in them often do not correspond. Often the seller's form contains terms different from or additional to those set forth in the buyer's form. Nevertheless, the parties proceed with the transaction. [Comment 1 was amended in 1966.]

2. Under this Article a proposed deal which in commercial understanding has in fact been closed is recognized as a contract. Therefore, any additional matter contained in the confirmation or in the acceptance falls within subsection (2) and must be regarded as a proposal for an added term unless the acceptance is made conditional on the acceptance of the additional or different terms. [Comment 2 was amended in 1966.]

3. Whether or not additional or different terms will become part of the agreement depends upon the provisions of subsection (2). If they are such as materially to alter the original bargain, they will not be included unless expressly agreed to by the other party. If, however, they are terms which would not so change the bargain they will be incorporated unless notice of objection to them has already been given or is given within a reasonable time.

4. Examples of typical clauses which would normally "materially alter" the contract and so result in surprise or hardship if incorporated without express awareness by the other party are: a clause negating such standard warranties as that of merchantability or fitness for a particular purpose in circumstances in which either warranty normally attaches; a clause requiring a guaranty of 90% or 100% deliveries in a case such as a contract by cannery, where the usage of the trade allows greater quantity leeways; a clause reserving to the seller the power to cancel upon the buyer's failure to meet any invoice when due; a clause requiring that complaints be made in a time materially shorter than customary or reasonable.

5. Examples of clauses which involve no element of unreasonable surprise and which therefore are to be incorporated in the contract unless notice of objection is seasonably given are: a clause setting forth and perhaps enlarging slightly upon the seller's exemption due to supervening causes beyond his control, similar to those covered by the provision of this Article on merchant's excuse by failure of presupposed conditions or a clause fixing in advance any reasonable formula of proration under such circumstances; a clause fixing a reasonable time for complaints within customary limits, or in the case of a purchase for sub-sale, providing for

inspection by the sub-purchaser; a clause providing for interest on overdue invoices or fixing the seller's standard credit terms where they are within the range of trade practice and do not limit any credit bargained for; a clause limiting the right of rejection for defects which fall within the customary trade tolerances for acceptance "with adjustment" or otherwise limiting remedy in a reasonable manner (see Sections 2–718 and 2–719).

6. If no answer is received within a reasonable time after additional terms are proposed, it is both fair and commercially sound to assume that their inclusion has been assented to. Where clauses on confirming forms sent by both parties conflict each party must be assumed to object to a clause of the other conflicting with one on the confirmation sent by himself. As a result the requirement that there be notice of objection which is found in subsection (2) is satisfied and the conflicting terms do not become a part of the contract. The contract then consists of the terms originally expressly agreed to, terms on which the confirmations agree, and terms supplied by this Act, including subsection (2). The written confirmation is also subject to Section 2–201. Under that section a failure to respond permits enforcement of a prior oral agreement; under this section a failure to respond permits additional terms to become part of the agreement. [Comment 6 was amended in 1966.]

7. In many cases, as where goods are shipped, accepted and paid for before any dispute arises, there is no question whether a contract has been made. In such cases, where the writings of the parties do not establish a contract, it is not necessary to determine which act or document constituted the offer and which the acceptance. See Section 2–204. The only question is what terms are included in the contract, and subsection (3) furnishes the governing rule. [Comment 7 was added in 1966.]

§ 2–208. Course of Performance or Practical Construction.

(1) Where the contract for sale involves repeated occasions for performance by either party with knowledge of the nature of the performance and opportunity for objection to it by the other, any course of performance accepted or acquiesced in without objection shall be relevant to determine the meaning of the agreement.

(2) The express terms of the agreement and any such course of performance, as well as any course of dealing and usage of trade, shall be construed whenever reasonable as consistent with each other; but when such construction is unreasonable, express terms shall control course of performance and course of performance shall control both course of dealing and usage of trade (Section 1–205).

(3) Subject to the provisions of the next section on modification and waiver, such course of performance shall be relevant to show a waiver or modification of any term inconsistent with such course of performance.

Official Comment

1. The parties themselves know best what they have meant by their words of agreement and their action under that agreement is the best indication of what that meaning was.

This section thus rounds out the set of factors which determines the meaning of the "agreement" and therefore also of the "unless otherwise agreed" qualification to various provisions of this Article....

3. Where it is difficult to determine whether a particular act merely sheds light on the meaning of the agreement or represents a waiver of a term of the agreement, the preference is in favor of "waiver" whenever such construction, plus the application of the provisions on the reinstatement of rights waived (see Section 2–209), is needed to preserve the flexible character of commercial contracts and to prevent surprise or other hardship....

§ 2–209. Modification, Rescission and Waiver.

(1) An agreement modifying a contract within this Article needs no consideration to be binding.

(2) A signed agreement which excludes modification or rescission except by a signed writing cannot be otherwise modified or rescinded, but except as between merchants such a requirement on a form supplied by the merchant must be separately signed by the other party.

(3) The requirements of the statute of frauds section of this Article (Section 2–201) must be satisfied if the contract as modified is within its provisions.

(4) Although an attempt at modification or rescission does not satisfy the requirements of subsection (2) or (3) it can operate as a waiver.

(5) A party who has made a waiver affecting an executory portion of the contract may retract the waiver by reasonable notification received by the other party that strict performance will be required of any term waived, unless the retraction would be unjust in view of a material change of position in reliance on the waiver.

Official Comment

1. This section seeks to protect and make effective all necessary and desirable modifications of sales contracts without regard to the technicalities which at present hamper such adjustments.

2. Subsection (1) provides that an agreement modifying a sales contract needs no consideration to be binding.

However, modifications made thereunder must meet the test of good faith imposed by this Act. The effective use of bad faith to escape performance on the original contract terms is barred, and the extortion of a "modification" without legitimate commercial reason is ineffective as a violation of the duty of good faith. Nor can a mere technical consideration support a modification made in bad faith.

The test of "good faith" between merchants or as against merchants includes "observance of reasonable commercial standards of fair dealing in the trade" (Section 2–103), and may in some situations require an objectively demonstrable reason for seeking a modification. But such matters as a market shift which makes performance come to involve a loss may provide such a reason even though there is no such unforeseen difficulty as would make out a legal excuse from performance under Sections 2–615 and 2–616.

3. Subsections (2) and (3) are intended to protect against false allegations of oral modifications....

The Statute of Frauds provisions of this Article are expressly applied to modifications by subsection (3). Under those provisions the "delivery and acceptance" test is limited to the goods which have been accepted, that is, to the past. "Modification" for the future cannot therefore be conjured up by oral testimony if the price involved is $500.00 or more since such modification must be shown at least by an authenticated memo. And since a memo is limited in its effect to the quantity of goods set forth in it there is safeguard against oral evidence.

Subsection (2) permits the parties in effect to make their own Statute of Frauds as regards any future modification of the contract by giving effect to a clause in a signed agreement which expressly requires any modification to be by signed writing. But note that if a consumer is to be held to such a clause on a form supplied by a merchant it must be separately signed.

4. Subsection (4) is intended, despite the provisions of subsections (2) and (3), to prevent contractual provisions excluding modification except by a signed writing from limiting in other respects the legal effect of the parties' actual later conduct. The effect of such conduct as a waiver is further regulated in subsection (5).

§ 2–210. Delegation of Performance; Assignment of Rights.

(1) A party may perform his duty through a delegate unless otherwise agreed or unless the other party has a substantial interest in having his original promisor perform or control the acts required by the contract. No delegation of performance relieves the party delegating of any duty to perform or any liability for breach.

(2) Unless otherwise agreed all rights of either seller or buyer can be assigned except where the assignment would materially change the duty of the other party, or increase materially the burden or risk imposed on him by his contract, or impair materially his chance of obtaining return performance. A right to damages for breach of the whole contract or a right arising out of the assignor's due performance of his entire obligation can be assigned despite agreement otherwise.

(3) Unless the circumstances indicate the contrary a prohibition of assignment of "the contract" is to be construed as barring only the delegation to the assignee of the assignor's performance.

(4) An assignment of "the contract" or of "all my rights under the contract" or an assignment in similar general terms is an assignment of rights and unless the language or the circumstances (as in an assignment for security) indicate the contrary, it is a delegation of performance of the duties of the assignor and its acceptance by the assignee constitutes a promise by him to perform those duties. This promise is enforceable by either the assignor or the other party to the original contract.

(5) The other party may treat any assignment which delegates performance as creating reasonable grounds for insecurity and may without prejudice to his rights against the assignor demand assurances from the assignee (Section 2–609).

Official Comment

1. Generally, this section recognizes both delegation of performance and assignability as normal and permissible incidents of a contract for the sale of goods. . . .

4. The nature of the contract or the circumstances of the case, however, may bar assignment of the contract even where delegation of performance is not involved. This Article and this section are intended to clarify this problem, particularly in cases dealing with output requirement and exclusive dealing contracts. In the first place the section on requirements and exclusive dealing removes from the construction of the original contract most of the "personal discretion" element by substituting the reasonably objective standard of good faith operation of the plant or business to be supplied. Secondly, the section on insecurity and assurances, which is specifically referred to in subsection (5) of this section, frees the other party from the doubts and uncertainty which may afflict him under an assignment of the character in

question by permitting him to demand adequate assurance of due performance without which he may suspend his own performance. Subsection (5) is not in any way intended to limit the effect of the section on insecurity and assurances and the word "performance" includes the giving of orders under a requirements contract. Of course, in any case where a material personal discretion is sought to be transferred, effective assignment is barred by subsection (2). . . .

7. This section is not intended as a complete statement of the law of delegation and assignment but is limited to clarifying a few points doubtful under the case law. Particularly, neither this section nor this Article touches directly on such questions as the need or effect of notice of the assignment, the rights of successive assignees, or any question of the form of an assignment, either as between the parties or as against any third parties. Some of these questions are dealt with in Article 9.

PART 3

GENERAL OBLIGATION AND CONSTRUCTION OF CONTRACT

§ 2–302. Unconscionable Contract or Clause.

(1) If the court as a matter of law finds the contract or any clause of the contract to have been unconscionable at the time it was made the court may refuse to enforce the contract, or it may enforce the remainder of the contract without the unconscionable clause, or it may so limit the application of any unconscionable clause as to avoid any unconscionable result.

(2) When it is claimed or appears to the court that the contract or any clause thereof may be unconscionable the parties shall be afforded a reasonable opportunity to present evidence as to its commercial setting, purpose and effect to aid the court in making the determination.

Official Comment

1. This section is intended to make it possible for the courts to police explicitly against the contracts or clauses which they find to be unconscionable. In the past such policing has been accomplished by adverse construction of language, by manipulation of the rules of offer and acceptance or by determinations that the clause is contrary to public policy or to the dominant purpose of the contract. This section is intended to allow the court to pass directly on the unconscionability of the contract or particular clause therein and to make a conclusion of law as to its unconscionability. The basic test is whether, in the light of the general commercial background and the commercial needs of the particular trade or case, the clauses involved are so one-sided as to be unconscionable under the circumstances existing at the time of the making of the contract. Subsection (2) makes it clear that it is proper for the court to hear evidence upon these questions. The principle is one of the prevention of oppression and unfair surprise (Cf. Campbell Soup Co. v. Wentz, 172 F.2d 80, 3d Cir. 1948) and not of disturbance of allocation of risks because of superior bargaining power. The underlying basis of this section is illustrated by the results in cases such as the following:

Kansas City Wholesale Grocery Co. v. Weber Packing Corporation, 93 Utah 414, 73 P.2d 1272 (1937), where a clause limiting time for complaints was held inapplicable to latent defects in a shipment of catsup which could be discovered only by microscopic analysis; Hardy v. General Motors Acceptance Corporation, 38 Ga.App. 463, 144 S.E. 327 (1928), holding that a disclaimer of warranty clause applied only to express warranties, thus letting in a fair implied warranty;

Andrews Bros. v. Singer & Co. (1934 CA) 1 K.B. 17, holding that where a car with substantial mileage was delivered instead of a "new" car, a disclaimer of warranties, including those "implied," left unaffected an "express obligation" on the description, even though the Sale of Goods Act called such an implied warranty; New Prague Flouring Mill Co. v. G. A. Spears, 194 Iowa 417, 189 N.W. 815 (1922), holding that a clause permitting the seller, upon the buyer's failure to supply shipping instructions, to cancel, ship, or allow delivery date to be indefinitely postponed 30 days at a time by the inaction, does not indefinitely postpone the date of measuring damages for the buyer's breach, to the seller's advantage; and Kansas Flour Mills Co. v. Dirks, 100 Kan. 376, 164 P. 273 (1917), where under a similar clause in a rising market the court permitted the buyer to measure his damages for non-delivery at the end of only one 30 day postponement; Green v. Arcos, Ltd. (1931 CA) 47 T.L.R. 336, where a blanket clause prohibiting rejection of shipments by the buyer was restricted to apply to shipments where discrepancies represented merely mercantile variations; Meyer v. Packard Cleveland Motor Co., 106 Ohio St. 328, 140 N.E. 118 (1922), in which the court held that a "waiver" of all agreements not specified did not preclude implied warranty of fitness of a rebuilt dump truck for ordinary use as a dump truck; Austin Co. v. J. H. Tillman Co., 104 Or. 541, 209 P. 131 (1922), where a clause limiting the buyer's remedy to return was held to be applicable only if the seller had delivered a machine needed for a construction job which reasonably met the contract description; Bekkevold v. Potts, 173 Minn.

87, 216 N.W. 790, 59 A.L.R. 1164 (1927), refusing to allow warranty of fitness for purpose imposed by law to be negated by clause excluding all warranties "made" by the seller; Robert A. Munroe & Co. v. Meyer (1930) 2 K.B. 312, holding that the warranty of description overrides a clause reading "with all faults and defects" where adulterated meat not up to the contract description was delivered.

2. Under this section the court, in its discretion, may refuse to enforce the contract as a whole if it is permeated by the unconscionability, or it may strike any single clause or group of clauses which are so tainted or which are contrary to the essential purpose of the agreement, or it may simply limit unconscionable clauses so as to avoid unconscionable results.

3. The present section is addressed to the court, and the decision is to be made by it. The commercial evidence referred to in subsection (2) is for the court's consideration, not the jury's. Only the agreement which results from the court's action on these matters is to be submitted to the general triers of the facts.

§ 2–305. Open Price Term.

(1) The parties if they so intend can conclude a contract for sale even though the price is not settled. In such a case the price is a reasonable price at the time for delivery if

    (a) nothing is said as to price; or

    (b) the price is left to be agreed by the parties and they fail to agree; or

    (c) the price is to be fixed in terms of some agreed market or other standard as set or recorded by a third person or agency and it is not so set or recorded.

(2) A price to be fixed by the seller or by the buyer means a price for him to fix in good faith.

(3) When a price left to be fixed otherwise than by agreement of the parties fails to be fixed through fault of one party the other may at his option treat the contract as cancelled or himself fix a reasonable price.

(4) Where, however, the parties intend not to be bound unless the price be fixed or agreed and it is not fixed or agreed there is no contract. In such a case the buyer must return any goods already received or if unable so to do must pay their reasonable value at the time of delivery and the seller must return any portion of the price paid on account.

Official Comment

1. This section applies when the price term is left open on the making of an agreement which is nevertheless intended by the parties to be a binding agreement. This Article rejects in these instances the formula that "an agreement to agree is unenforceable" if the case falls within subsection (1) of this section, and rejects also defeating such agreements on the ground of "indefiniteness". Instead this Article recognizes the dominant intention of the parties to have the deal continue to be binding upon both. As to future performance, since this Article recog-

nizes remedies such as cover (Section 2–712), resale (Section 2–706) and specific performance (Section 2–716) which go beyond any mere arithmetic as between contract price and market price, there is usually a "reasonably certain basis for granting an appropriate remedy for breach" so that the contract need not fail for indefiniteness.

2. Under some circumstances the postponement of agreement on price will mean that no deal has really been concluded, and this is made express in the preamble of subsection (1) ("The parties *if they so intend*") and in subsection (4). Whether or not this is so is, in most cases, a question to be determined by the trier of fact.

3. Subsection (2), dealing with the situation where the price is to be fixed by one party rejects the uncommercial idea that an agreement that the seller may fix the price means

that he may fix any price he may wish by the express qualification that the price so fixed must be fixed in good faith. Good faith includes observance of reasonable commercial standards of fair dealing in the trade if the party is a merchant. (Section 2–103). But in the normal case a "posted price" or a future seller's or buyer's "given price," "price in effect," "market price," or the like satisfies the good faith requirement.

4. The section recognizes that there may be cases in which a particular person's judgment is not chosen merely as a barometer or index of a fair price but is an essential condition to the parties' intent to make any contract at all. . . .

6. Throughout the entire section, the purpose is to give effect to the agreement which has been made. . . .

§ 2–306. Output, Requirements and Exclusive Dealings.

(1) A term which measures the quantity by the output of the seller or the requirements of the buyer means such actual output or requirements as may occur in good faith, except that no quantity unreasonably disproportionate to any stated estimate or in the absence of a stated estimate to any normal or otherwise comparable prior output or requirements may be tendered or demanded.

(2) A lawful agreement by either the seller or the buyer for exclusive dealing in the kind of goods concerned imposes unless otherwise agreed an obligation by the seller to use best efforts to supply the goods and by the buyer to use best efforts to promote their sale.

Official Comment

1. Subsection (1) of this section, in regard to output and requirements, applies to this specific problem the general approach of this Act which requires the reading of commercial background and intent into the language of any agreement and demands good faith in the performance of that agreement. It applies to such contracts of nonproducing establishments

such as dealers or distributors as well as to manufacturing concerns.

2. Under this Article, a contract for output or requirements is not too indefinite since it is held to mean the actual good faith output or requirements of the particular party. Nor does such a contract lack mutuality of obligation since, under this section, the party who will determine quantity

31

is required to operate his plant or conduct his business in good faith and according to commercial standards of fair dealing in the trade so that his output or requirements will approximate a reasonably foreseeable figure. Reasonable elasticity in the requirements is expressly envisaged by this section and good faith variations from prior requirements are permitted even when the variation may be such as to result in discontinuance. A shut-down by a requirements buyer for lack of orders might be permissible when a shut-down merely to curtail losses would not. The essential test is whether the party is acting in good faith. Similarly, a sudden expansion of the plant by which requirements are to be measured would not be included within the scope of the contract as made but normal expansion undertaken in good faith would be within the scope of this section. One of the factors in an expansion situation would be whether the market price had risen greatly in a case in which the requirements contract contained a fixed price. . . .

3. If an estimate of output or requirements is included in the agreement, no quantity unreasonably disproportionate to it may be tendered or demanded. Any minimum or maximum set by the agreement shows a clear limit on the intended elasticity. In similar fashion, the agreed estimate is to be regarded as a center around which the parties intend the variation to occur. . . .

5. Subsection (2), on exclusive dealing, makes explicit the commercial rule embodied in this Act under which the parties to such contracts are held to have impliedly, even when not expressly, bound themselves to use reasonable diligence as well as good faith in their performance of the contract. Under such contracts the exclusive agent is required, although no express commitment has been made, to use reasonable effort and due diligence in the expansion of the market or the promotion of the product, as the case may be. The principal is expected under such a contract to refrain from supplying any other dealer or agent within the exclusive territory. An exclusive dealing agreement brings into play all of the good faith aspects of the output and requirement problems of subsection (1). It also raises questions of insecurity and right to adequate assurance under this Article.

§ 2–307. Delivery in Single Lot or Several Lots.

Unless otherwise agreed all goods called for by a contract for sale must be tendered in a single delivery and payment is due only on such tender but where the circumstances give either party the right to make or demand delivery in lots the price if it can be apportioned may be demanded for each lot.

Official Comment

. . .

2. Where the actual agreement or the circumstances do not indicate otherwise, delivery in lots is not permitted under this section and the buyer is properly entitled to reject for a deficiency in the tender, subject to any privilege in the seller to cure the tender.

3. The "but" clause of this section goes to the case in which it is not commercially feasible to deliver or to receive the goods in a single lot as for example, where a contract calls for

the shipment of ten carloads of coal and only three cars are available at a given time. Similarly, in a contract involving brick necessary to build a building the buyer's storage space may be limited so that it would be impossible to receive the entire amount of brick at once, or it may be necessary to assemble the goods as in the case of cattle on the range, or to mine them....

4. Where the circumstances indicate that a party has a right to delivery in lots, the price may be demanded for each lot if it is apportionable.

§ 2–309. Absence of Specific Time Provisions; Notice of Termination.

(1) The time for shipment or delivery or any other action under a contract if not provided in this Article or agreed upon shall be a reasonable time.

(2) Where the contract provides for successive performances but is indefinite in duration it is valid for a reasonable time but unless otherwise agreed may be terminated at any time by either party.

(3) Termination of a contract by one party except on the happening of an agreed event requires that reasonable notification be received by the other party and an agreement dispensing with notification is invalid if its operation would be unconscionable.

Official Comment

. . .

7. Subsection (2) applies a commercially reasonable view to resolve the conflict which has arisen in the cases as to contracts of indefinite duration. The "reasonable time" of duration appropriate to a given arrangement is limited by the circumstances. When the arrangement has been carried on by the parties over the years, the "reasonable time" can continue indefinitely and the contract will not terminate until notice.

8. Subsection (3) recognizes that the application of principles of good faith and sound commercial practice normally call for such notification of the termination of a going contract relationship as will give the other party reasonable time to seek a substitute arrangement....

10. The requirement of notification is dispensed with where the contract provides for termination on the happening of an "agreed event." "Event" is a term chosen here to contrast with "option" or the like.

§ 2–310. Open Time for Payment or Running of Credit....

Unless otherwise agreed

(a) payment is due at the time and place at which the buyer is to receive the goods even though the place of shipment is the place of delivery; and

(b) if the seller is authorized to send the goods he may ship them under reservation, and may tender the documents of title, but the buyer may inspect the goods after their arrival before payment is due unless such inspection is inconsistent with the terms of the contract (Section 2–513); ....

§ 2–311. Options and Cooperation Respecting Performance.

(1) An agreement for sale which is otherwise sufficiently definite (subsection (3) of Section 2–204) to be a contract is not made invalid by the fact that it leaves particulars of performance to be specified by one of the parties. Any such specification must be made in good faith and within limits set by commercial reasonableness. . . .

§ 2–312. Warranty of Title and Against Infringement; Buyer's Obligation Against Infringement.

(1) Subject to subsection (2) there is in a contract for sale a warranty by the seller that

  (a) the title conveyed shall be good, and its transfer rightful; and

  (b) the goods shall be delivered free from any security interest or other lien or encumbrance of which the buyer at the time of contracting has no knowledge.

(2) A warranty under subsection (1) will be excluded or modified only by specific language or by circumstances which give the buyer reason to know that the person selling does not claim title in himself or that he is purporting to sell only such right or title as he or a third person may have.

(3) Unless otherwise agreed a seller who is a merchant regularly dealing in goods of the kind warrants that the goods shall be delivered free of the rightful claim of any third person by way of infringement or the like but a buyer who furnishes specifications to the seller must hold the seller harmless against any such claim which arises out of compliance with the specifications.

§ 2–313. Express Warranties by Affirmation, Promise, Description, Sample.

(1) Express warranties by the seller are created as follows:

  (a) Any affirmation of fact or promise made by the seller to the buyer which relates to the goods and becomes part of the basis of the bargain creates an express warranty that the goods shall conform to the affirmation or promise.

  (b) Any description of the goods which is made part of the basis of the bargain creates an express warranty that the goods shall conform to the description.

  (c) Any sample or model which is made part of the basis of the bargain creates an express warranty that the whole of the goods shall conform to the sample or model.

(2) It is not necessary to the creation of an express warranty that the seller use formal words such as "warrant" or "guarantee" or that he have a specific intention to make a warranty, but an affirmation merely of the value of the goods or a statement purporting to be merely the seller's opinion or commendation of the goods does not create a warranty.

Official Comment

1. "Express" warranties rest on "dickered" aspects of the individual bargain, and go so clearly to the essence of that bargain that words of disclaimer in a form are repugnant to the basic dickered terms. "Implied" warranties rest so clearly on a common factual situation or set of conditions that no particular language or action is necessary to evidence them and they will arise in such a situation unless unmistakably negated....

2. Although this section is limited in its scope and direct purpose to warranties made by the seller to the buyer as part of a contract for sale, the warranty sections of this Article are not designed in any way to disturb those lines of case law growth which have recognized that warranties need not be confined either to sales contracts or to the direct parties to such a contract. They may arise in other appropriate circumstances such as in the case of bailments for hire.... The provisions of Section 2–318 on third party beneficiaries expressly recognize this case law development within one particular area. Beyond that, the matter is left to the case law with the intention that the policies of this Act may offer useful guidance in dealing with further cases as they arise.

3. The present section deals with affirmations of fact by the seller, descriptions of the goods or exhibitions of samples, exactly as any other part of a negotiation which ends in a contract is dealt with. No specific intention to make a warranty is necessary if any of these factors is made part of the basis of the bargain. In actual practice affirmations of fact made by the seller about the goods during a bargain are regarded as part of the description of those goods; hence no particular reliance on such statements need be shown in order to weave them into the fabric of the agreement. Rather, any fact which is to take such affirmations, once made, out of the agreement requires clear affirmative proof. The issue normally is one of fact.

4. In view of the principle that the whole purpose of the law of warranty is to determine what it is that the seller has in essence agreed to sell, the policy is adopted of those cases which refuse except in unusual circumstances to recognize a material deletion of the seller's obligation. Thus, a contract is normally a contract for a sale of something describable and described. A clause generally disclaiming "all warranties, express or implied" cannot reduce the seller's obligation with respect to such description and therefore cannot be given literal effect under Section 2–316.

This is not intended to mean that the parties, if they consciously desire, cannot make their own bargain as they wish. But in determining what they have agreed upon good faith is a factor and consideration should be given to the fact that the probability is small that a real price is intended to be exchanged for a pseudo-obligation....

6. The basic situation as to statements affecting the true essence of the bargain is no different when a sample or model is involved in the transaction....

Although the underlying principles are unchanged, the facts are often ambiguous when something is shown as illustrative, rather than as a straight sample. In general, the presumption is that any sample or model just as any affirmation of fact is intended to become a basis of the bargain. But there is no escape from the question of fact.... The question is whether the seller has so acted with reference to the sample as to make him responsible that the whole shall have at least the values shown by it....

7. The precise time when words of description or affirmation are made or samples are shown is not material. The sole question is whether the language or samples or models are fairly to be regarded as part of the contract. If language is used after the closing of the deal (as when the buyer when taking delivery asks and receives an additional assurance), the warranty becomes a modification, and need not be supported by consideration if it is otherwise reasonable and in order (Section 2–209).

8. Concerning affirmations of value or a seller's opinion or commendation under subsection (2), the basic question remains the same: What statements of the seller have in the circumstances and in objective judgment become part of the basis of the bargain? As indicated above, all of the statements of the seller do so unless good reason is shown to the contrary. The provisions of subsection (2) are included, however, since common experience discloses that some statements or predictions cannot fairly be viewed as entering into the bargain. Even as to false statements of value, however, the possibility is left open that a remedy may be provided by the law relating to fraud or misrepresentation.

§ 2–314. Implied Warranty: Merchantability; Usage of Trade.

(1) Unless excluded or modified (Section 2–316), a warranty that the goods shall be merchantable is implied in a contract for their sale if the seller is a merchant with respect to goods of that kind. Under this section the serving for value of food or drink to be consumed either on the premises or elsewhere is a sale.

(2) Goods to be merchantable must be at least such as

    (a) pass without objection in the trade under the contract description; and

    (b) in the case of fungible goods, are of fair average quality within the description; and

    (c) are fit for the ordinary purposes for which such goods are used; and

    (d) run, within the variations permitted by the agreement, of even kind, quality and quantity within each unit and among all units involved; and

    (e) are adequately contained, packaged, and labeled as the agreement may require; and

    (f) conform to the promise or affirmations of fact made on the container or label if any.

(3) Unless excluded or modified (Section 2–316) other implied warranties may arise from course of dealing or usage of trade.

Official Comment

. . .

2. The question when the warranty is imposed turns basically on the meaning of the terms of the agreement as recognized in the trade. Goods delivered under an agreement made by a merchant in a given line of trade must be of a quality comparable to that generally acceptable in that line of trade under the description or other designation of the goods used in the agreement. The responsibility imposed rests on any merchant-seller. . . . A contract for the sale of second-hand goods, however, involves only such obligation as is appropriate to such goods for that is their contract description. . . .

6. Subsection (2) does not purport to exhaust the meaning of "merchantable" nor to negate any of its attributes not specifically mentioned in the text of the statute, but arising by usage of trade or through case law. The language used is "must be at least such as . . .," and the intention is to leave open other possible attributes of merchantability.

7. Paragraphs (a) and (b) of subsection (2) are to be read together. Both refer, as indicated above, to the standards of that line of the trade which fits the transaction and the seller's business. "Fair average" is a term directly appropriate to agricultural bulk products and means goods centering around the middle belt of quality, not the least or the worst that can be understood in the particular trade by the designation, but such as can pass "without objection." Of course a fair percentage of the least is permissible but the goods are not "fair average" if they are all of the least or worst quality possible under the description. In cases of doubt as to what quality is intended, the price at which a merchant closes a contract is an excellent index of the nature and scope of his obligation under the present section.

8. Fitness for the ordinary purposes for which goods of the type are used is a fundamental concept of the present section and is covered in paragraph (c). As stated above, merchantability is also a part of the obligation owing to the purchaser for use. Correspondingly, protection, under this aspect of the warranty, of the person buying for resale to the ultimate consumer is equally necessary, and merchantable goods must therefore be "honestly" resalable in the normal course of business because they are what they purport to be. . . .

12. Subsection (3) is to make explicit that usage of trade and course of dealing can create warranties and that they are implied rather than express warranties and thus subject to exclusion or modification under Section 2–316. A typical instance would be the obligation to provide pedigree papers to evidence conformity of the animal to the contract in the case of a pedigreed dog or blooded bull. . . .

§ 2–315. Implied Warranty: Fitness for Particular Purpose.

Where the seller at the time of contracting has reason to know any particular purpose for which the goods are required and that the buyer is relying on the seller's skill or judgment to select or furnish suitable goods, there is unless excluded or modified under the next section an implied warranty that the goods shall be fit for such purpose.

Official Comment

1. Whether or not this warranty arises in any individual case is basically a question of fact to be determined by the circumstances of the contracting. Under this section the buyer need not bring home to the seller actual knowledge of the particular purpose for which the goods are intended or of his reliance on the seller's skill and judgment, if the circumstances are such that the seller has reason to realize the purpose intended or that the reliance exists. The buyer, of course, must actually be relying on the seller.

2. A "particular purpose" differs from the ordinary purpose for which the goods are used in that it envisages a specific use by the buyer which is peculiar to the nature of his business whereas the ordinary purposes for which goods are used are those envisaged in the concept of merchantability and go to uses which are customarily made of the goods in question. For example, shoes are generally used for the purpose of walking upon ordinary ground, but a seller may know that a particular pair was selected to be used for climbing mountains.

A contract may of course include both a warranty of merchantability and one of fitness for a particular purpose.

The provisions of this Article on the cumulation and conflict of express and implied warranties must be considered on the question of inconsistency between or among warranties. In such a case any question of fact as to which warranty was intended by the parties to apply must be resolved in favor of the warranty of fitness for particular purpose as against all other warranties except where the buyer has taken upon himself the responsibility of furnishing the technical specifications.

... Although normally the warranty will arise only where the seller is a merchant with the appropriate "skill or judgment," it can arise as to non-merchants where this is justified by the particular circumstances.

5. ... Under the present section the existence of a patent or other trade name and the designation of the article by that name, or indeed in any other definite manner, is only one of the facts to be considered on the question of whether the buyer actually relied on the seller, but it is not of itself decisive of the issue. If the buyer himself is insisting on a particular brand he is not relying on the seller's skill and judgment and so no warranty results. ...

§ 2–316. Exclusion or Modification of Warranties.

(1) Words or conduct relevant to the creation of an express warranty and words or conduct tending to negate or limit warranty shall be construed wherever reasonable as consistent with each other; but subject to the provisions of this Article on parol or extrinsic evidence (Section 2–202) negation or limitation is inoperative to the extent that such construction is unreasonable.

(2) Subject to subsection (3), to exclude or modify the implied warranty of merchantability or any part of it the language must mention merchantability and in case of a writing must be conspicuous, and to exclude or modify any implied warranty of fitness the exclusion must be by a writing and conspicuous. Language to exclude all implied warranties of fitness is

sufficient if it states, for example, that "There are no warranties which extend beyond the description on the face hereof."

(3) Notwithstanding subsection (2)

(a) unless the circumstances indicate otherwise, all implied warranties are excluded by expressions like "as is", "with all faults" or other language which in common understanding calls the buyer's attention to the exclusion of warranties and makes plain that there is no implied warranty; and

(b) when the buyer before entering into the contract has examined the goods or the sample or model as fully as he desired or has refused to examine the goods there is no implied warranty with regard to defects which an examination ought in the circumstances to have revealed to him; and

(c) an implied warranty can also be excluded or modified by course of dealing or course of performance or usage of trade.

(4) Remedies for breach of warranty can be limited in accordance with the provisions of this Article on liquidation or limitation of damages and on contractual modification of remedy (Sections 2–718 and 2–719).

Official Comment

1. This section is designed principally to deal with those frequent clauses in sales contracts which seek to exclude "all warranties, express or implied." It seeks to protect a buyer from unexpected and unbargained language of disclaimer by denying effect to such language when inconsistent with language of express warranty and permitting the exclusion of implied warranties only by conspicuous language or other circumstances which protect the buyer from surprise.

2. The seller is protected under this Article against false allegations of oral warranties by its provisions on parol and extrinsic evidence and against unauthorized representations by the customary "lack of authority" clauses. This Article treats the limitation or avoidance of consequential damages as a matter of limiting reme-dies for breach, separate from the matter of creation of liability under a warranty. If no warranty exists, there is of course no problem of limiting remedies for breach of warranty. Under subsection (4) the question of limitation of remedy is governed by the sections referred to rather than by this section....

7. Paragraph (a) of subsection (3) deals with general terms such as "as is," "as they stand," "with all faults," and the like. Such terms in ordinary commercial usage are understood to mean that the buyer takes the entire risk as to the quality of the goods involved. The terms covered by paragraph (a) are in fact merely a particularization of paragraph (c) which provides for exclusion or modification of implied warranties by usage of trade....

§ 2–317. Cumulation and Conflict of Warranties Express or Implied.

Warranties whether express or implied shall be construed as consistent with each other and as cumulative, but if such construction is unreasonable the intention of the parties shall determine which warranty is dominant. In ascertaining that intention the following rules apply:

    (a) Exact or technical specifications displace an inconsistent sample or model or general language of description.

    (b) A sample from an existing bulk displaces inconsistent general language of description.

    (c) Express warranties displace inconsistent implied warranties other than an implied warranty of fitness for a particular purpose.

Official Comment

1. The present section rests on the basic policy of this Article that no warranty is created except by some conduct (either affirmative action or failure to disclose) on the part of the seller. Therefore, all warranties are made cumulative unless this construction of the contract is impossible or unreasonable. . . .

2. The rules of this section are designed to aid in determining the intention of the parties as to which of inconsistent warranties which have arisen from the circumstances of their transaction shall prevail. These rules of intention are to be applied only where factors making for an equitable estoppel of the seller do not exist and where he has in perfect good faith made warranties which later turn out to be inconsistent. To the extent that the seller has led the buyer to believe that all of the warranties can be performed, he is estopped from setting up any essential inconsistency as a defense. . . .

§ 2–318. Third Party Beneficiaries of Warranties Express or Implied.

Note: *If this Act is introduced in the Congress of the United States this section should be omitted. (States to select one alternative.)*

Alternative A

A seller's warranty whether express or implied extends to any natural person who is in the family or household of his buyer or who is a guest in his home if it is reasonable to expect that such person may use, consume or be affected by the goods and who is injured in person by breach of the warranty. A seller may not exclude or limit the operation of this section.

Alternative B

A seller's warranty whether express or implied extends to any natural person who may reasonably be expected to use, consume or be affected by the goods and who is injured in person by breach of the warranty. A seller may not exclude or limit the operation of this section.

Alternative C

A seller's warranty whether express or implied extends to any person who may reasonably be expected to use, consume or be affected by the goods and who is injured by breach of the warranty. A seller may not exclude or limit the operation of this section with respect to injury to the person of an individual to whom the warranty extends.

As amended in 1966.

Official Comment

1. The last sentence of this section does not mean that a seller is precluded from excluding or disclaiming a warranty which might otherwise arise in connection with the sale provided such exclusion or modification is permitted by Section 2–316. Nor does that sentence preclude the seller from limiting the remedies of his own buyer and of any beneficiaries, in any manner provided in Sections 2–718 or 2–719. To the extent that the contract of sale contains provisions under which warranties are excluded or modified, or remedies for breach are limited, such provisions are equally operative against beneficiaries of warranties under this section. What this last sentence forbids is exclusion of liability by the seller to the persons to whom the warranties which he has made to his buyer would extend under this section.

2. The purpose of this section is to give certain beneficiaries the benefit of the same warranty which the buyer received in the contract of sale, thereby freeing any such beneficiaries from any technical rules as to "privity." It seeks to accomplish this purpose without any derogation of any right or remedy resting on negligence....

§ 2–328. Sale by Auction.

(1) In a sale by auction if goods are put up in lots each lot is the subject of a separate sale.

(2) A sale by auction is complete when the auctioneer so announces by the fall of the hammer or in other customary manner. Where a bid is made while the hammer is falling in acceptance of a prior bid the auctioneer may in his discretion reopen the bidding or declare the goods sold under the bid on which the hammer was falling.

(3) Such a sale is with reserve unless the goods are in explicit terms put up without reserve. In an auction with reserve the auctioneer may withdraw the goods at any time until he announces completion of the sale. In an auction without reserve, after the auctioneer calls for bids on an article or lot, that article or lot cannot be withdrawn unless no bid is made within a reasonable time. In either case a bidder may retract his bid until the auctioneer's announcement of completion of the sale, but a bidder's retraction does not revive any previous bid.

(4) If the auctioneer knowingly receives a bid on the seller's behalf or the seller makes or procures such a bid, and notice has not been given that liberty for such bidding is reserved, the buyer may at his option avoid the sale or take the goods at the price of the last good faith bid prior to the completion of the sale. This subsection shall not apply to any bid at a forced sale.

PART 5

PERFORMANCE

§ 2–501. Insurable Interest in Goods; Manner of Identification of Goods.

(1) The buyer obtains a special property and an insurable interest in goods by identification of existing goods as goods to which the contract refers even though the goods so identified are non-conforming and he has an option to return or reject them. Such identification can be made at any time and in any manner explicitly agreed to by the parties. In the absence of explicit agreement identification occurs

    (a) when the contract is made if it is for the sale of goods already existing and identified;

    (b) if the contract is for the sale of future goods other than those described in paragraph (c), when goods are shipped, marked or otherwise designated by the seller as goods to which the contract refers;

    (c) when the crops are planted or otherwise become growing crops or the young are conceived if the contract is for the sale of unborn young to be born within twelve months after contracting or for the sale of crops to be harvested within twelve months or the next normal harvest season after contracting whichever is longer . . . .

§ 2–503. Manner of Seller's Tender of Delivery.

(1) Tender of delivery requires that the seller put and hold conforming goods at the buyer's disposition and give the buyer any notification reasonably necessary to enable him to take delivery. The manner, time and place for tender are determined by the agreement and this Article, and in particular

    (a) tender must be at a reasonable hour, and if it is of goods they must be kept available for the period reasonably necessary to enable the buyer to take possession; but

    (b) unless otherwise agreed the buyer must furnish facilities reasonably suited to the receipt of the goods . . . .

§ 2–507. Effect of Seller's Tender; Delivery on Condition.

(1) Tender of delivery is a condition to the buyer's duty to accept the goods and, unless otherwise agreed, to his duty to pay for them. Tender entitles the seller to acceptance of the goods and to payment according to the contract.

(2) Where payment is due and demanded on the delivery to the buyer of goods or documents of title, his right as against the seller to retain or dispose of them is conditional upon his making the payment due.

§ 2–508. Cure by Seller of Improper Tender or Delivery; Replacement.

(1) Where any tender or delivery by the seller is rejected because non-conforming and the time for performance has not yet expired, the seller may seasonably notify the buyer of his intention to cure and may then within the contract time make a conforming delivery.

(2) Where the buyer rejects a non-conforming tender which the seller had reasonable grounds to believe would be acceptable with or without money allowance the seller may if he seasonably notifies the buyer have a further reasonable time to substitute a conforming tender.

Official Comment

1. Subsection (1) permits a seller who has made a non-conforming tender in any case to make a conforming delivery within the contract time upon seasonable notification to the buyer. It applies even where the seller has taken back the non-conforming goods and refunded the purchase price. He may still make a good tender within the contract period. The closer, however, it is to the contract date, the greater is the necessity for extreme promptness on the seller's part in notifying of his intention to cure, if such notification is to be "seasonable" under this subsection.

The rule of this subsection, moreover, is qualified by its underlying reasons. Thus if, after contracting for June delivery, a buyer later makes known to the seller his need for shipment early in the month and the seller ships accordingly, the "contract time" has been cut down by the supervening modification and the time for cure of tender must be referred to this modified time term.

2. Subsection (2) seeks to avoid injustice to the seller by reason of a surprise rejection by the buyer. However, the seller is not protected unless he had "reasonable grounds to believe" that the tender would be acceptable. Such reasonable grounds can lie in prior course of dealing, course of performance or usage of trade as well as in the particular circumstances surrounding the making of the contract. The seller is charged with commercial knowledge of any factors in a particular sales situation which require him to comply strictly with his obligations under the contract as, for example, strict conformity of documents in an overseas shipment or the sale of precision parts or chemicals for use in manufacture. Further, if the buyer gives notice either implicitly, as by a prior course of dealing involving rigorous inspections, or expressly, as by the deliberate inclusion of a "no replacement" clause in the contract, the seller is to be held to rigid compliance. If the clause appears in a "form" contract evidence that it is out of line with trade usage or the prior course of dealing and was not called to the seller's attention may be sufficient to show that the seller had reasonable grounds to believe that the tender would be acceptable.

3. The words "a further reasonable time to substitute a conforming

tender" are intended as words of limitation to protect the buyer. What is a "reasonable time" depends upon the attending circumstances....

4. Existing trade usages permitting variations without rejection but with price allowance enter into the agreement itself as contractual limitations of remedy and are not covered by this section.

§ 2–509. Risk of Loss in the Absence of Breach.

(1) Where the contract requires or authorizes the seller to ship the goods by carrier

    (a) if it does not require him to deliver them at a particular destination, the risk of loss passes to the buyer when the goods are duly delivered to the carrier even though the shipment is under reservation (Section 2–505); but

    (b) if it does require him to deliver them at a particular destination and the goods are there duly tendered while in the possession of the carrier, the risk of loss passes to the buyer when the goods are there duly so tendered as to enable the buyer to take delivery.

(2) Where the goods are held by a bailee to be delivered without being moved, the risk of loss passes to the buyer

    (a) on his receipt of a negotiable document of title covering the goods; or

    (b) on acknowledgment by the bailee of the buyer's right to possession of the goods; or

    (c) after his receipt of a non-negotiable document of title or other written direction to deliver, as provided in subsection (4)(b) of Section 2–503.

(3) In any case not within subsection (1) or (2), the risk of loss passes to the buyer on his receipt of the goods if the seller is a merchant; otherwise the risk passes to the buyer on tender of delivery.

(4) The provisions of this section are subject to contrary agreement of the parties and to the provisions of this Article on sale on approval (Section 2–327) and on effect of breach on risk of loss (Section 2–510).

Official Comment

1. The underlying theory of these sections on risk of loss is the adoption of the contractual approach rather than an arbitrary shifting of the risk with the "property" in the goods. The scope of the present section, therefore, is limited strictly to those cases where there has been no breach by the seller. Where for any reason his delivery or tender fails to conform to the contract, the present section does not apply and the situation is governed by the provisions on effect of breach on risk of loss....

§ 2–510. Effect of Breach on Risk of Loss.

(1) Where a tender or delivery of goods so fails to conform to the contract as to give a right of rejection the risk of their loss remains on the seller until cure or acceptance.

(2) Where the buyer rightfully revokes acceptance he may to the extent of any deficiency in his effective insurance coverage treat the risk of loss as having rested on the seller from the beginning.

(3) Where the buyer as to conforming goods already identified to the contract for sale repudiates or is otherwise in breach before risk of their loss has passed to him, the seller may to the extent of any deficiency in his effective insurance coverage treat the risk of loss as resting on the buyer for a commercially reasonable time.

§ 2–511. Tender of Payment by Buyer; Payment by Check.

(1) Unless otherwise agreed tender of payment is a condition to the seller's duty to tender and complete any delivery.

(2) Tender of payment is sufficient when made by any means or in any manner current in the ordinary course of business unless the seller demands payment in legal tender and gives any extension of time reasonably necessary to procure it.

(3) Subject to the provisions of this Act on the effect of an instrument on an obligation (Section 3–802), payment by check is conditional and is defeated as between the parties by dishonor of the check on due presentment.

As amended in 1994.

§ 2–513. Buyer's Right to Inspection of Goods.

(1) Unless otherwise agreed and subject to subsection (3), where goods are tendered or delivered or identified to the contract for sale, the buyer has a right before payment or acceptance to inspect them at any reasonable place and time and in any reasonable manner. When the seller is required or authorized to send the goods to the buyer, the inspection may be after their arrival.

(2) Expenses of inspection must be borne by the buyer but may be recovered from the seller if the goods do not conform and are rejected....

PART 6

BREACH, REPUDIATION AND EXCUSE

§ 2–601. Buyer's Rights on Improper Delivery.

Subject to the provisions of this Article on breach in installment contracts (Section 2–612) and unless otherwise agreed under the sections on contractual limitations of remedy (Sections 2–718 and 2–719), if the goods or the tender of delivery fail in any respect to conform to the contract, the buyer may

    (a) reject the whole; or

    (b) accept the whole; or

(c) accept any commercial unit or units and reject the rest.

Official Comment

1. A buyer accepting a non-conforming tender is not penalized by the loss of any remedy otherwise open to him. This policy extends to cover and regulate the acceptance of a part of any lot improperly tendered in any case where the price can reasonably be apportioned. Partial acceptance is permitted whether the part of the goods accepted conforms or not. The only limitation on partial acceptance is that good faith and commercial reasonableness must be used to avoid undue impairment of the value of the remaining portion of the goods. This is the reason for the insistence on the "commercial unit" in paragraph (c)....

2. Acceptance made with the knowledge of the other party is final. An original refusal to accept may be withdrawn by a later acceptance if the seller has indicated that he is holding the tender open. However, if the buyer attempts to accept, either in whole or in part, after his original rejection has caused the seller to arrange for other disposition of the goods, the buyer must answer for any ensuing damage since the next section provides that any exercise of ownership after rejection is wrongful as against the seller. Further, he is liable even though the seller may choose to treat his action as acceptance rather than conversion, since the damage flows from the misleading notice. Such arrangements for resale or other disposition of the goods by the seller must be viewed as within the normal contemplation of a buyer who has given notice of rejection. However, the buyer's attempts in good faith to dispose of defective goods where the seller has failed to give instructions within a reasonable time are not to be regarded as an acceptance.

§ 2–602. Manner and Effect of Rightful Rejection.

(1) Rejection of goods must be within a reasonable time after their delivery or tender. It is ineffective unless the buyer seasonably notifies the seller.

(2) Subject to the provisions of the two following sections on rejected goods (Sections 2–603 and 2–604),

    (a) after rejection any exercise of ownership by the buyer with respect to any commercial unit is wrongful as against the seller; and

    (b) if the buyer has before rejection taken physical possession of goods in which he does not have a security interest under the provisions of this Article (subsection (3) of Section 2–711), he is under a duty after rejection to hold them with reasonable care at the seller's disposition for a time sufficient to permit the seller to remove them; but

    (c) the buyer has no further obligations with regard to goods rightfully rejected.

(3) The seller's rights with respect to goods wrongfully rejected are governed by the provisions of this Article on Seller's remedies in general (Section 2–703).

Official Comment

1. A tender or delivery of goods made pursuant to a contract of sale, even though wholly non-conforming, requires affirmative action by the buyer to avoid acceptance. Under subsection (1), therefore, the buyer is given a reasonable time to notify the seller of his rejection, but without such seasonable notification his rejection is ineffective....

2. Subsection (2) lays down the normal duties of the buyer upon rejection, which flow from the relationship of the parties. Beyond his duty to hold the goods with reasonable care for the buyer's [seller's] disposition, this section continues the policy of prior uniform legislation in generally relieving the buyer from any duties with respect to them, except when the circumstances impose the limited obligation of salvage upon him under the next section.

3. The present section applies only to rightful rejection by the buyer. If the seller has made a tender which in all respects conforms to the contract, the buyer has a positive duty to accept and his failure to do so constitutes a "wrongful rejection" which gives the seller immediate remedies for breach. Subsection (3) is included here to emphasize the sharp distinction between the rejection of an improper tender and the non-acceptance which is a breach by the buyer.

§ 2–605. Waiver of Buyer's Objections by Failure to Particularize.

(1) The buyer's failure to state in connection with rejection a particular defect which is ascertainable by reasonable inspection precludes him from relying on the unstated defect to justify rejection or to establish breach

   (a) where the seller could have cured it if stated seasonably; or

   (b) between merchants when the seller has after rejection made a request in writing for a full and final written statement of all defects on which the buyer proposes to rely.

(2) Payment against documents made without reservation of rights precludes recovery of the payment for defects apparent on the face of the documents.

Official Comment

1. The present section rests upon a policy of permitting the buyer to give a quick and informal notice of defects in a tender without penalizing him for omissions in his statement, while at the same time protecting a seller who is reasonably misled by the buyer's failure to state curable defects.

2. Where the defect in a tender is one which could have been cured by the seller, a buyer who merely rejects the delivery without stating his objections to it is probably acting in commercial bad faith and seeking to get out of a deal which has become unprofitable. Subsection (1)(a), following the general policy of this Article

47

which looks to preserving the deal wherever possible, therefore insists that the seller's right to correct his tender in such circumstances be protected. . . .

4. Subsection (2) applies to the particular case of documents the same principle which the section on effects of acceptance applies to the case of goods. . . .

§ 2–606. What Constitutes Acceptance of Goods.

(1) Acceptance of goods occurs when the buyer

    (a) after a reasonable opportunity to inspect the goods signifies to the seller that the goods are conforming or that he will take or retain them in spite of their non-conformity; or

    (b) fails to make an effective rejection (subsection (1) of Section 2–602), but such acceptance does not occur until the buyer has had a reasonable opportunity to inspect them; or

    (c) does any act inconsistent with the seller's ownership; but if such act is wrongful as against the seller it is an acceptance only if ratified by him.

(2) Acceptance of a part of any commercial unit is acceptance of that entire unit.

§ 2–607. Effect of Acceptance; Notice of Breach; Burden of Establishing Breach After Acceptance. . . .

(1) The buyer must pay at the contract rate for any goods accepted.

(2) Acceptance of goods by the buyer precludes rejection of the goods accepted and if made with knowledge of a non-conformity cannot be revoked because of it unless the acceptance was on the reasonable assumption that the non-conformity would be seasonably cured but acceptance does not of itself impair any other remedy provided by this Article for non-conformity.

(3) Where a tender has been accepted

    (a) the buyer must within a reasonable time after he discovers or should have discovered any breach notify the seller of breach or be barred from any remedy; . . . .

(4) The burden is on the buyer to establish any breach with respect to the goods accepted. . . .

§ 2–608. Revocation of Acceptance in Whole or in Part.

(1) The buyer may revoke his acceptance of a lot or commercial unit whose non-conformity substantially impairs its value to him if he has accepted it

    (a) on the reasonable assumption that its non-conformity would be cured and it has not been seasonably cured; or

    (b) without discovery of such non-conformity if his acceptance was reasonably induced either by the difficulty of discovery before acceptance or by the seller's assurances.

(2) Revocation of acceptance must occur within a reasonable time after the buyer discovers or should have discovered the ground for it and before any substantial change in condition of the goods which is not caused by their own defects. It is not effective until the buyer notifies the seller of it.

(3) A buyer who so revokes has the same rights and duties with regard to the goods involved as if he had rejected them.

Official Comment

1. Although the prior basic policy is continued, the buyer is no longer required to elect between revocation of acceptance and recovery of damages for breach. Both are now available to him. The non-alternative character of the two remedies is stressed by the terms used in the present section. The section no longer speaks of "rescission," a term capable of ambiguous application either to transfer of title to the goods or to the contract of sale and susceptible also of confusion with cancellation for cause of an executed or executory portion of the contract. The remedy under this section is instead referred to simply as "revocation of acceptance" of goods tendered under a contract for sale and involves no suggestion of "election" of any sort....

3. "Assurances" by the seller under paragraph (b) of subsection (1) can rest as well in the circumstances or in the contract as in explicit language used at the time of delivery. The reason for recognizing such assurances is that they induce the buyer to delay discovery....

§ 2–609. Right to Adequate Assurance of Performance.

(1) A contract for sale imposes an obligation on each party that the other's expectation of receiving due performance will not be impaired. When reasonable grounds for insecurity arise with respect to the performance of either party the other may in writing demand adequate assurance of due performance and until he receives such assurance may if commercially reasonable suspend any performance for which he has not already received the agreed return.

(2) Between merchants the reasonableness of grounds for insecurity and the adequacy of any assurance offered shall be determined according to commercial standards.

(3) Acceptance of any improper delivery or payment does not prejudice the aggrieved party's right to demand adequate assurance of future performance.

(4) After receipt of a justified demand failure to provide within a reasonable time not exceeding thirty days such assurance of due performance as is adequate under the circumstances of the particular case is a repudiation of the contract.

Official Comment

1. The section rests on the recognition of the fact that the essential purpose of a contract between commercial men is actual performance and they do not bargain merely for a promise, or for a promise plus the right to win a lawsuit and that a continuing sense of reliance and security that the promised performance will be forthcoming when due, is an important feature of the bargain. If either the willingness or the ability of a party to perform declines materially between the time of contracting and the time for performance, the other party is threatened with the loss of a substantial part of what he has bargained for....

2. Three measures have been adopted to meet the needs of commercial men in such situations. First, the aggrieved party is permitted to suspend his own performance and any preparation therefor, with excuse for any resulting necessary delay, until the situation has been clarified. "Suspend performance" under this section means to hold up performance pending the outcome of the demand, and includes also the holding up of any preparatory action....

Secondly, the aggrieved party is given the right to require adequate assurance that the other party's performance will be duly forthcoming. This principle is reflected in the familiar clauses permitting the seller to curtail deliveries if the buyer's credit becomes impaired, which when held within the limits of reasonableness and good faith actually express no more than the fair business meaning of any commercial contract.

Third, and finally, this section provides the means by which the aggrieved party may treat the contract as broken if his reasonable grounds for insecurity are not cleared up within a reasonable time. This is the principle underlying the law of anticipatory breach, whether by way of defective part performance or by repudiation. The present section merges these three principles of law and commercial practice into a single theory of general application to all sales agreements looking to future performance.

3. Subsection (2) of the present section requires that "reasonable" grounds and "adequate" assurance as used in subsection (1) be defined by commercial rather than legal standards....

Under commercial standards and in accord with commercial practice, a ground for insecurity need not arise from or be directly related to the contract in question. The law as to "dependence" or "independence" of promises within a single contract does not control the application of the present section.

Thus a buyer who falls behind in "his account" with the seller, even though the items involved have to do with separate and legally distinct contracts, impairs the seller's expectation of due performance....

The nature of the sales contract enters also into the question of reasonableness. For example, a report from an apparently trustworthy source that the seller had shipped defective goods or was planning to ship them would normally give the buyer reasonable grounds for insecurity....

4. What constitutes "adequate" assurance of due performance is subject to the same test of factual conditions. For example, where the buyer can make use of a defective delivery, a mere promise by a seller of good repute that he is giving the matter his attention and that the defect will not

be repeated, is normally sufficient. Under the same circumstances, however, a similar statement by a known corner-cutter might well be considered insufficient without the posting of a guaranty or, if so demanded by the buyer, a speedy replacement of the delivery involved. By the same token where a delivery has defects, even though easily curable, which interfere with easy use by the buyer, no verbal assurance can be deemed adequate which is not accompanied by replacement, repair, money-allowance, or other commercially reasonable cure....

5. A failure to provide adequate assurance of performance and thereby to re-establish the security of expectation, results in a breach only "by repudiation" under subsection (4). Therefore, the possibility is continued of retraction of the repudiation under the section dealing with that problem, unless the aggrieved party has acted on the breach in some manner.

The thirty day limit on the time to provide assurance is laid down to free the question of reasonable time from uncertainty in later litigation.

§ 2–610. Anticipatory Repudiation.

When either party repudiates the contract with respect to a performance not yet due the loss of which will substantially impair the value of the contract to the other, the aggrieved party may

(a) for a commercially reasonable time await performance by the repudiating party; or

(b) resort to any remedy for breach (Section 2–703 or Section 2–711), even though he has notified the repudiating party that he would await the latter's performance and has urged retraction; and

(c) in either case suspend his own performance or proceed in accordance with the provisions of this Article on the seller's right to identify goods to the contract notwithstanding breach or to salvage unfinished goods (Section 2–704).

Official Comment

1. With the problem of insecurity taken care of by the preceding section and with provision being made in this Article as to the effect of a defective delivery under an installment contract, anticipatory repudiation centers upon an overt communication of intention or an action which renders performance impossible or demonstrates a clear determination not to continue with performance.

Under the present section when such a repudiation substantially impairs the value of the contract, the aggrieved party may at any time resort to his remedies for breach, or he may suspend his own performance while he negotiates with, or awaits performance by, the other party. But if he awaits performance beyond a commercially reasonable time he cannot recover resulting damages which he should have avoided.

2. It is not necessary for repudiation that performance be made literally and utterly impossible. Repudiation can result from action which reasonably indicates a rejection of the continuing obligation. And, a repudiation automatically results under the preceding section on insecurity when a party fails to provide adequate as-

surance of due future performance within thirty days after a justifiable demand therefor has been made. Under the language of this section, a demand by one or both parties for more than the contract calls for in the way of counter-performance is not in itself a repudiation nor does it invalidate a plain expression of desire for future performance. However, when under a fair reading it amounts to a statement of intention not to perform except on conditions which go beyond the contract, it becomes a repudiation.

3. The test chosen to justify an aggrieved party's action under this section is the same as that in the section on breach in installment contracts—namely the substantial value of the contract....

§ 2–611. Retraction of Anticipatory Repudiation.

(1) Until the repudiating party's next performance is due he can retract his repudiation unless the aggrieved party has since the repudiation cancelled or materially changed his position or otherwise indicated that he considers the repudiation final.

(2) Retraction may be by any method which clearly indicates to the aggrieved party that the repudiating party intends to perform, but must include any assurance justifiably demanded under the provisions of this Article (Section 2–609).

(3) Retraction reinstates the repudiating party's rights under the contract with due excuse and allowance to the aggrieved party for any delay occasioned by the repudiation.

§ 2–612. "Installment Contract"; Breach.

(1) An "installment contract" is one which requires or authorizes the delivery of goods in separate lots to be separately accepted, even though the contract contains a clause "each delivery is a separate contract" or its equivalent.

(2) The buyer may reject any installment which is non-conforming if the non-conformity substantially impairs the value of that installment and cannot be cured or if the non-conformity is a defect in the required documents; but if the non-conformity does not fall within subsection (3) and the seller gives adequate assurance of its cure the buyer must accept that installment.

(3) Whenever non-conformity or default with respect to one or more installments substantially impairs the value of the whole contract there is a breach of the whole. But the aggrieved party reinstates the contract if he accepts a non-conforming installment without seasonably notifying of cancellation or if he brings an action with respect only to past installments or demands performance as to future installments.

Official Comment

1. The definition of an installment contract is phrased more broadly in this Article so as to cover installment deliveries tacitly authorized by the circumstances or by the option of either party.

2. In regard to the apportionment of the price for separate payment this Article applies the more liberal test of what can be apportioned rather than the test of what is clearly apportioned by the agreement.... A provision for separate payment for each lot delivered ordinarily means that the price is at least roughly calculable by units of quantity, but such a provision is not essential to an "installment contract." If separate acceptance of separate deliveries is contemplated, no generalized contrast between wholly "entire" and wholly "divisible" contracts has any standing under this Article.

3. This Article rejects any approach which gives clauses such as "each delivery is a separate contract" their legalistically literal effect. Such contracts nonetheless call for installment deliveries....

4. One of the requirements for rejection under subsection (2) is nonconformity substantially impairing the value of the installment in question. However, an installment agreement may require accurate conformity in quality as a condition to the right to acceptance if the need for such conformity is made clear either by express provision or by the circumstances. In such a case the effect of the agreement is to define explicitly what amounts to substantial impairment of value impossible to cure. A clause requiring accurate compliance as a condition to the right to acceptance must, however, have some basis in reason, must avoid imposing hardship by surprise and is subject to waiver or to displacement by practical construction.

Substantial impairment of the value of an installment can turn not only on the quality of the goods but also on such factors as time, quantity, assortment, and the like. It must be judged in terms of the normal or specifically known purposes of the contract....

5. Under subsection (2) an installment delivery must be accepted if the non-conformity is curable and the seller gives adequate assurance of cure. Cure of non-conformity of an installment in the first instance can usually be afforded by an allowance against the price, or in the case of reasonable discrepancies in quantity either by a further delivery or a partial rejection. This Article requires reasonable action by a buyer in regard to discrepant delivery and good faith requires that the buyer make any reasonable minor outlay of time or money necessary to cure an overshipment by severing out an acceptable percentage thereof. The seller must take over a cure which involves any material burden; the buyer's obligation reaches only to cooperation. Adequate assurance for purposes of subsection (2) is measured by the same standards as under the section on right to adequate assurance of performance.

6. Subsection (3) is designed to further the continuance of the contract in the absence of an overt cancellation. The question arising when an action is brought as to a single installment only is resolved by making such action waive the right to cancellation. This involves merely a defect in one or more installments, as contrasted with the situation where there is a true repudiation within the section on anticipatory repudiation. Whether the non-conformity in any given installment justifies cancellation as to the future depends, not on whether such non-conformity indicates an intent or likelihood that the future deliveries will also be defective, but whether the non-conformity substantially impairs the value of the whole contract. If only the seller's security in regard to future installments is impaired, he has the right to demand adequate assurances of prop-

er future performance but has not an immediate right to cancel the entire contract. It is clear under this Article, however, that defects in prior installments are cumulative in effect, so that acceptance does not wash out the defect "waived." Prior policy is continued, putting the rule as to buyer's default on the same footing as that in regard to seller's default....

§ 2–613. Casualty to Identified Goods.

Where the contract requires for its performance goods identified when the contract is made, and the goods suffer casualty without fault of either party before the risk of loss passes to the buyer, or in a proper case under a "no arrival, no sale" term (Section 2–324) then

    (a) if the loss is total the contract is avoided; and

    (b) if the loss is partial or the goods have so deteriorated as no longer to conform to the contract the buyer may nevertheless demand inspection and at his option either treat the contract as avoided or accept the goods with due allowance from the contract price for the deterioration or the deficiency in quantity but without further right against the seller.

§ 2–614. Substituted Performance.

(1) Where without fault of either party the agreed berthing, loading, or unloading facilities fail or an agreed type of carrier becomes unavailable or the agreed manner of delivery otherwise becomes commercially impracticable but a commercially reasonable substitute is available, such substitute performance must be tendered and accepted.

(2) If the agreed means or manner of payment fails because of domestic or foreign governmental regulation, the seller may withhold or stop delivery unless the buyer provides a means or manner of payment which is commercially a substantial equivalent. If delivery has already been taken, payment by the means or in the manner provided by the regulation discharges the buyer's obligation unless the regulation is discriminatory, oppressive or predatory.

Official Comment

1. Subsection (1) requires the tender of a commercially reasonable substituted performance where agreed to facilities have failed or become commercially impracticable. Under this Article, in the absence of specific agreement, the normal or usual facilities enter into the agreement either through the circumstances, usage of trade or prior course of dealing.

This section appears between Section 2–613 on casualty to identified goods and the next section on excuse by failure of presupposed conditions, both of which deal with excuse and complete avoidance of the contract where the occurrence or non-occurrence of a contingency which was a basic assumption of the contract makes the expected performance impossible. The distinction between the present section and those sections lies in whether the failure or impossibility of performance arises in connection with an incidental matter or goes to the very heart of the agreement. The differing lines of solution are contrasted in a comparison of International Paper Co. v. Rockefeller, 161 App.Div. 180, 146 N.Y.S. 371 (1914) and Meyer v. Sullivan, 40 Cal.App. 723, 181 P. 847 (1919). In the former case a contract for the sale of spruce to be cut from a particular tract of land was involved. When a fire destroyed the trees growing on that tract the seller was held excused since performance was impossible. In the latter case the contract called for delivery of wheat "f.o.b. Kosmos Steamer at Seattle." The war led to cancellation of that line's sailing schedule after space had been duly engaged and the buyer was held entitled to demand substituted delivery at the warehouse on the line's loading dock. . . .

There must, however, be a true commercial impracticability to excuse the agreed to performance and justify a substituted performance. When this is the case a reasonable substituted performance tendered by either party should excuse him from strict compliance with contract terms which do not go to the essence of the agreement. . . .

§ 2–615. Excuse by Failure of Presupposed Conditions.

Except so far as a seller may have assumed a greater obligation and subject to the preceding section on substituted performance:

    (a) Delay in delivery or non-delivery in whole or in part by a seller who complies with paragraphs (b) and (c) is not a breach of his duty under a contract for sale if performance as agreed has been made impracticable by the occurrence of a contingency the non-occurrence of which was a basic assumption on which the contract was made or by compliance in good faith with any applicable foreign or domestic governmental regulation or order whether or not it later proves to be invalid.

    (b) Where the causes mentioned in paragraph (a) affect only a part of the seller's capacity to perform, he must allocate production and deliveries among his customers but may at his option include regular customers not then under contract as well as his own requirements for further manufacture. He may so allocate in any manner which is fair and reasonable.

    (c) The seller must notify the buyer seasonably that there will be delay or non-delivery and, when allocation is required under paragraph (b), of the estimated quota thus made available for the buyer.

Official Comment

1. This section excuses a seller from timely delivery of goods contracted for, where his performance has become commercially impracticable because of unforeseen supervening circumstances not within the contemplation of the parties at the time of contracting. The destruction of specific goods and the problem of the use of substituted performance on points other than delay or quantity, treated elsewhere in this Article, must be distinguished from the matter covered by this section.

2. The present section deliberately refrains from any effort at an exhaustive expression of contingencies and is to be interpreted in all cases sought to be brought within its scope

in terms of its underlying reason and purpose.

3. The first test for excuse under this Article in terms of basic assumption is a familiar one. The additional test of commercial impracticability (as contrasted with "impossibility," "frustration of performance" or "frustration of the venture") has been adopted in order to call attention to the commercial character of the criterion chosen by this Article.

4. Increased cost alone does not excuse performance unless the rise in cost is due to some unforeseen contingency which alters the essential nature of the performance. Neither is a rise or a collapse in the market in itself a justification, for that is exactly the type of business risk which business contracts made at fixed prices are intended to cover. But a severe shortage of raw materials or of supplies due to a contingency such as war, embargo, local crop failure, unforeseen shutdown of major sources of supply or the like, which either causes a marked increase in cost or altogether prevents the seller from securing supplies necessary to his performance, is within the contemplation of this section. . . .

5. Where a particular source of supply is exclusive under the agreement and fails through casualty, the present section applies rather than the provision on destruction or deterioration of specific goods. The same holds true where a particular source of supply is shown by the circumstances to have been contemplated or assumed by the parties at the time of contracting. . . . There is no excuse under this section, however, unless the seller has employed all due measures to assure himself that his source will not fail. . . .

In the case of failure of production by an agreed source for causes beyond the seller's control, the seller should, if possible, be excused since production by an agreed source is without more a basic assumption of the contract. . . .

7. The failure of conditions which go to convenience or collateral values rather than to the commercial practicability of the main performance does not amount to a complete excuse. However, good faith and the reason of the present section and of the preceding one may properly be held to justify and even to require any needed delay involved in a good faith inquiry seeking a readjustment of the contract terms to meet the new conditions.

8. The provisions of this section are made subject to assumption of greater liability by agreement and such agreement is to be found not only in the expressed terms of the contract but in the circumstances surrounding the contracting, in trade usage and the like. Thus the exemptions of this section do not apply when the contingency in question is sufficiently foreshadowed at the time of contracting to be included among the business risks which are fairly to be regarded as part of the dickered terms, either consciously or as a matter of reasonable, commercial interpretation from the circumstances. . . .

9. The case of a farmer who has contracted to sell crops to be grown on designated land may be regarded as falling either within the section on casualty to identified goods or this section, and he may be excused, when there is a failure of the specific crop, either on the basis of the destruction of identified goods or because of the failure of a basic assumption of the contract.

Exemption of the buyer in the case of a "requirements" contract is covered by the "Output and Requirements" section both as to assumption and allocation of the relevant risks. But when a contract by a manufacturer to buy fuel or raw material makes no specific reference to a particular venture and no such reference may be drawn from the circumstances, commercial understanding views it as a general deal in the general market and not conditioned on any assumption of the continuing operation of the buyer's plant....

10. Following its basic policy of using commercial practicability as a test for excuse, this section recognizes as of equal significance either a foreign or domestic regulation and disregards any technical distinctions between "law," "regulation," "order" and the like. Nor does it make the present action of the seller depend upon the eventual judicial determination of the legality of the particular governmental action. The seller's good faith belief in the validity of the regulation is the test under this Article and the best evidence of his good faith is the general commercial acceptance of the regulation. However, governmental interference cannot excuse unless it truly "supervenes" in such a manner as to be beyond the seller's assumption of risk. And any action by the party claiming excuse which causes or colludes in inducing the governmental action preventing his performance would be in breach of good faith and would destroy his exemption.

11. An excused seller must fulfill his contract to the extent which the supervening contingency permits, and if the situation is such that his customers are generally affected he must take account of all in supplying one. Subsections (a) and (b), therefore, explicitly permit in any proration a fair and reasonable attention to the needs of regular customers who are probably relying on spot orders for supplies....

§ 2–616. Procedure on Notice Claiming Excuse.

(1) Where the buyer receives notification of a material or indefinite delay or an allocation justified under the preceding section he may by written notification to the seller as to any delivery concerned, and where the prospective deficiency substantially impairs the value of the whole contract under the provisions of this Article relating to breach of installment contracts (Section 2–612), then also as to the whole,

      (a) terminate and thereby discharge any unexecuted portion of the contract; or

      (b) modify the contract by agreeing to take his available quota in substitution.

(2) If after receipt of such notification from the seller the buyer fails so to modify the contract within a reasonable time not exceeding thirty days the contract lapses with respect to any deliveries affected.

(3) The provisions of this section may not be negated by agreement except in so far as the seller has assumed a greater obligation under the preceding section.

PART 7

REMEDIES

§ 2–702. Seller's Remedies on Discovery of Buyer's Insolvency.

(1) Where the seller discovers the buyer to be insolvent he may refuse delivery except for cash including payment for all goods theretofore delivered under the contract, and stop delivery under this Article (Section 2–705)....

§ 2–703. Seller's Remedies in General.

Where the buyer wrongfully rejects or revokes acceptance of goods or fails to make a payment due on or before delivery or repudiates with respect to a part or the whole, then with respect to any goods directly affected and, if the breach is of the whole contract (Section 2–612), then also with respect to the whole undelivered balance, the aggrieved seller may

   (a) withhold delivery of such goods;

   (b) stop delivery by any bailee as hereafter provided (Section 2–705);

   (c) proceed under the next section respecting goods still unidentified to the contract;

   (d) resell and recover damages as hereafter provided (Section 2–706);

   (e) recover damages for non-acceptance (Section 2–708) or in a proper case the price (Section 2–709);

   (f) cancel.

Official Comment

1. This section is an index section which gathers together in one convenient place all of the various remedies open to a seller for any breach by the buyer. This Article rejects any doctrine of election of remedy as a fundamental policy and thus the remedies are essentially cumulative in nature and include all of the available remedies for breach. Whether the pursuit of one remedy bars another depends entirely on the facts of the individual case....

4. It should also be noted that this Act requires its remedies to be liberally administered and provides that any right or obligation which it declares is enforceable by action unless a different effect is specifically prescribed (Section 1–106).

§ 2–704. Seller's Right to Identify Goods to the Contract Notwithstanding Breach or to Salvage Unfinished Goods.

(1) An aggrieved seller under the preceding section may

   (a) identify to the contract conforming goods not already identified if at the time he learned of the breach they are in his possession or control;

(b) treat as the subject of resale goods which have demonstrably been intended for the particular contract even though those goods are unfinished.

(2) Where the goods are unfinished an aggrieved seller may in the exercise of reasonable commercial judgment for the purposes of avoiding loss and of effective realization either complete the manufacture and wholly identify the goods to the contract or cease manufacture and resell for scrap or salvage value or proceed in any other reasonable manner.

§ 2–706. Seller's Resale Including Contract for Resale.

(1) Under the conditions stated in Section 2–703 on seller's remedies, the seller may resell the goods concerned or the undelivered balance thereof. Where the resale is made in good faith and in a commercially reasonable manner the seller may recover the difference between the resale price and the contract price together with any incidental damages allowed under the provisions of this Article (Section 2–710), but less expenses saved in consequence of the buyer's breach.

(2) Except as otherwise provided in subsection (3) or unless otherwise agreed resale may be at public or private sale including sale by way of one or more contracts to sell or of identification to an existing contract of the seller. Sale may be as a unit or in parcels and at any time and place and on any terms but every aspect of the sale including the method, manner, time, place and terms must be commercially reasonable. The resale must be reasonably identified as referring to the broken contract, but it is not necessary that the goods be in existence or that any or all of them have been identified to the contract before the breach.

(3) Where the resale is at private sale the seller must give the buyer reasonable notification of his intention to resell.

(4) Where the resale is at public sale

(a) only identified goods can be sold except where there is a recognized market for a public sale of futures in goods of the kind; and

(b) it must be made at a usual place or market for public sale if one is reasonably available and except in the case of goods which are perishable or threaten to decline in value speedily the seller must give the buyer reasonable notice of the time and place of the resale; and

(c) if the goods are not to be within the view of those attending the sale the notification of sale must state the place where the goods are located and provide for their reasonable inspection by prospective bidders; and

(d) the seller may buy.

(5) A purchaser who buys in good faith at a resale takes the goods free of any rights of the original buyer even though the seller fails to comply with one or more of the requirements of this section.

(6) The seller is not accountable to the buyer for any profit made on any resale. A person in the position of a seller (Section 2–707) or a buyer who has rightfully rejected or justifiably revoked acceptance must account for any excess over the amount of his security interest, as hereinafter defined (subsection (3) of Section 2–711).

Official Comment

. . .

2. In order to recover the damages prescribed in subsection (1) the seller must act "in good faith and in a commercially reasonable manner" in making the resale. . . . Failure to act properly under this section deprives the seller of the measure of damages here provided and relegates him to that provided in Section 2–708.

Under this Article the seller resells by authority of law, in his own behalf, for his own benefit and for the purpose of fixing his damages. The theory of a seller's agency is thus rejected.

3. If the seller complies with the prescribed standard of duty in making the resale, he may recover from the buyer the damages provided for in subsection (1). Evidence of market or current prices at any particular time or place is relevant only on the question of whether the seller acted in a commercially reasonable manner in making the resale. . . .

The distinction drawn by some courts between cases where the title had not passed to the buyer and the seller had resold as owner, and cases where the title had passed and the seller had resold by virtue of his lien on the goods, is rejected.

4. Subsection (2) frees the remedy of resale from legalistic restrictions and enables the seller to resell in accordance with reasonable commercial practices so as to realize as high a price as possible in the circumstances. By "public" sale is meant a sale by auction. A "private" sale may be effected by solicitation and negotiation conducted either directly or through a broker. . . .

§ 2–708. Seller's Damages for Non-acceptance or Repudiation.

(1) Subject to subsection (2) and to the provisions of this Article with respect to proof of market price (Section 2–723), the measure of damages for non-acceptance or repudiation by the buyer is the difference between the market price at the time and place for tender and the unpaid contract price together with any incidental damages provided in this Article (Section 2–710), but less expenses saved in consequence of the buyer's breach.

(2) If the measure of damages provided in subsection (1) is inadequate to put the seller in as good a position as performance would have done then the measure of damages is the profit (including reasonable overhead) which the seller would have made from full performance by the buyer, together with any incidental damages provided in this Article (Section 2–710), due allowance for costs reasonably incurred and due credit for payments or proceeds of resale.

Official Comment

. . .

2. The provision of this section permitting recovery of expected profit including reasonable overhead where the standard measure of damages is inadequate, together with the new requirement that price actions may be sustained only where resale is impractical, are designed to eliminate the unfair and economically wasteful results arising under the older law when fixed price articles were involved.

This section permits the recovery of lost profits in all appropriate cases, which would include all standard priced goods. The normal measure there would be list price less cost to the dealer or list price less manufacturing cost to the manufacturer. It is not necessary to a recovery of "profit" to show a history of earnings, especially if a new venture is involved.

3. In all cases the seller may recover incidental damages.

§ 2–709. Action for the Price.

(1) When the buyer fails to pay the price as it becomes due the seller may recover, together with any incidental damages under the next section, the price

    (a) of goods accepted or of conforming goods lost or damaged within a commercially reasonable time after risk of their loss has passed to the buyer; and

    (b) of goods identified to the contract if the seller is unable after reasonable effort to resell them at a reasonable price or the circumstances reasonably indicate that such effort will be unavailing.

(2) Where the seller sues for the price he must hold for the buyer any goods which have been identified to the contract and are still in his control except that if resale becomes possible he may resell them at any time prior to the collection of the judgment. The net proceeds of any such resale must be credited to the buyer and payment of the judgment entitles him to any goods not resold.

(3) After the buyer has wrongfully rejected or revoked acceptance of the goods or has failed to make a payment due or has repudiated (Section 2–610), a seller who is held not entitled to the price under this section shall nevertheless be awarded damages for non-acceptance under the preceding section.

Official Comment

. . .

2. The action for the price is now generally limited to those cases where resale of the goods is impracticable except where the buyer has accepted the goods or where they have been destroyed after risk of loss has passed to the buyer. . . .

6. This section is intended to be exhaustive in its enumeration of cases where an action for the price lies.

7. If the action for the price fails, the seller may nonetheless have proved a case entitling him to damages for non-acceptance. In such a situation, subsection (3) permits recovery of those damages in the same action.

§ 2–710. Seller's Incidental Damages.

Incidental damages to an aggrieved seller include any commercially reasonable charges, expenses or commissions incurred in stopping delivery, in the transportation, care and custody of goods after the buyer's breach, in connection with return or resale of the goods or otherwise resulting from the breach.

§ 2–711. Buyer's Remedies in General; Buyer's Security Interest in Rejected Goods.

(1) Where the seller fails to make delivery or repudiates or the buyer rightfully rejects or justifiably revokes acceptance then with respect to any goods involved, and with respect to the whole if the breach goes to the whole contract (Section 2–612), the buyer may cancel and whether or not he has done so may in addition to recovering so much of the price as has been paid

    (a) "cover" and have damages under the next section as to all the goods affected whether or not they have been identified to the contract; or

    (b) recover damages for non-delivery as provided in this Article (Section 2–713).

(2) Where the seller fails to deliver or repudiates the buyer may also

    (a) if the goods have been identified recover them as provided in this Article (Section 2–502); or

    (b) in a proper case obtain specific performance or replevy the goods as provided in this Article (Section 2–716).

(3) On rightful rejection or justifiable revocation of acceptance a buyer has a security interest in goods in his possession or control for any payments made on their price and any expenses reasonably incurred in their inspection, receipt, transportation, care and custody and may hold such goods and resell them in like manner as an aggrieved seller (Section 2–706).

Official Comment

1. To index in this section the buyer's remedies, subsection (1) covering those remedies permitting the recovery of money damages, and subsection (2) covering those which permit reaching the goods themselves. The remedies listed here are those available to a buyer who has not accepted the goods or who has justifiably revoked his acceptance. The remedies available to a buyer with regard to goods finally accepted ap-

pear in the section dealing with breach in regard to accepted goods. The buyer's right to proceed as to all goods when the breach is as to only some of the goods is determined by the section on breach in installment contracts and by the section on partial acceptance.

Despite the seller's breach, proper retender of delivery under the section on cure of improper tender or replacement can effectively preclude the buyer's remedies under this section, except for any delay involved. . . .

§ 2–712. "Cover"; Buyer's Procurement of Substitute Goods.

(1) After a breach within the preceding section the buyer may "cover" by making in good faith and without unreasonable delay any reasonable purchase of or contract to purchase goods in substitution for those due from the seller.

(2) The buyer may recover from the seller as damages the difference between the cost of cover and the contract price together with any incidental or consequential damages as hereinafter defined (Section 2–715), but less expenses saved in consequence of the seller's breach.

(3) Failure of the buyer to effect cover within this section does not bar him from any other remedy.

Official Comment

1. This section provides the buyer with a remedy aimed at enabling him to obtain the goods he needs thus meeting his essential need. This remedy is the buyer's equivalent of the seller's right to resell.

2. The definition of "cover" under subsection (1) envisages a series of contracts or sales, as well as a single contract or sale; goods not identical with those involved but commercially usable as reasonable substitutes under the circumstances of the particular case; and contracts on credit or delivery terms differing from the contract in breach, but again reasonable under the circumstances. The test of proper cover is whether at the time and place the buyer acted in good faith and in a reasonable manner, and it is immaterial that hindsight may later prove that the method of cover used was not the cheapest or most effective.

The requirement that the buyer must cover "without unreasonable delay" is not intended to limit the time necessary for him to look around and decide as to how he may best effect cover. The test here is similar to that generally used in this Article as to reasonable time and seasonable action.

3. Subsection (3) expresses the policy that cover is not a mandatory remedy for the buyer. The buyer is always free to choose between cover and damages for non-delivery under the next section.

However, this subsection must be read in conjunction with the section which limits the recovery of consequential damages to such as could not have been obviated by cover. Moreover, the operation of the section on specific performance of contracts for "unique" goods must be considered in this connection for availability of the goods to the particular buyer for his particular needs is the test for that remedy and inability to cover is made an express condition to the right of the buyer to replevy the goods.

4. This section does not limit cover to merchants, in the first instance. It is the vital and important remedy for the consumer buyer as well. Both are free to use cover: the domestic or non-merchant consumer is required only to act in normal good faith while the merchant buyer must also observe all reasonable commercial standards of fair dealing in the trade, since this falls within the definition of good faith on his part.

§ 2-713. Buyer's Damages for Non-delivery or Repudiation.

(1) Subject to the provisions of this Article with respect to proof of market price (Section 2-723), the measure of damages for non-delivery or repudiation by the seller is the difference between the market price at the time when the buyer learned of the breach and the contract price together with any incidental and consequential damages provided in this Article (Section 2-715), but less expenses saved in consequence of the seller's breach.

(2) Market price is to be determined as of the place for tender or, in cases of rejection after arrival or revocation of acceptance, as of the place of arrival.

Official Comment

1. The general baseline adopted in this section uses as a yardstick the market in which the buyer would have obtained cover had he sought that relief. So the place for measuring damages is the place of tender (or the place of arrival if the goods are rejected or their acceptance is revoked after reaching their destination) and the crucial time is the time at which the buyer learns of the breach. . . .

5. The present section provides a remedy which is completely alternative to cover under the preceding section and applies only when and to the extent that the buyer has not covered.

§ 2-714. Buyer's Damages for Breach in Regard to Accepted Goods.

(1) Where the buyer has accepted goods and given notification (subsection (3) of Section 2-607) he may recover as damages for any non-conformity of tender the loss resulting in the ordinary course of events from the seller's breach as determined in any manner which is reasonable.

(2) The measure of damages for breach of warranty is the difference at the time and place of acceptance between the value of the goods accepted and the value they would have had if they had been as warranted, unless special circumstances show proximate damages of a different amount.

(3) In a proper case any incidental and consequential damages under the next section may also be recovered.

Official Comment

Prior Uniform Statutory Provision: Section 69(6) and (7), Uniform Sales Act.

Changes: Rewritten.

Purposes of Changes:

1. This section deals with the remedies available to the buyer after the goods have been accepted and the time for revocation of acceptance has gone by. . . .

2. The "non-conformity" referred to in subsection (1) includes not only breaches of warranties but also any failure of the seller to perform according to his obligations under the contract. . . .

3. Subsection (2) describes the usual, standard and reasonable method of ascertaining damages in the case of breach of warranty but it is not intended as an exclusive measure. . . .

§ 2–715. Buyer's Incidental and Consequential Damages.

(1) Incidental damages resulting from the seller's breach include expenses reasonably incurred in inspection, receipt, transportation and care and custody of goods rightfully rejected, any commercially reasonable charges, expenses or commissions in connection with effecting cover and any other reasonable expense incident to the delay or other breach.

(2) Consequential damages resulting from the seller's breach include

    (a) any loss resulting from general or particular requirements and needs of which the seller at the time of contracting had reason to know and which could not reasonably be prevented by cover or otherwise; and

    (b) injury to person or property proximately resulting from any breach of warranty.

Official Comment

1. Subsection (1) is intended to provide reimbursement for the buyer who incurs reasonable expenses in connection with the handling of rightfully rejected goods or goods whose acceptance may be justifiably revoked, or in connection with effecting cover where the breach of the contract lies in non-conformity or non-delivery of the goods. The incidental damages listed are not intended to be exhaustive but are merely illustrative of the typical kinds of incidental damage.

2. Subsection (2) operates to allow the buyer, in an appropriate case, any consequential damages which are the result of the seller's breach. The "tacit agreement" test for the recovery of consequential damages is rejected. Although the older rule at common law which made the seller liable for all consequential damages of which he had "reason to know" in advance is followed, the liberality of that rule is modified by refusing to permit recovery unless the buyer could not reasonably have prevented the loss by cover or otherwise. Subparagraph (2) carries forward the provisions of the prior uniform statutory provision as to consequential damages resulting from breach of warranty,

but modifies the rule by requiring first that the buyer attempt to minimize his damages in good faith, either by cover or otherwise.

3. In the absence of excuse under the section on merchant's excuse by failure of presupposed conditions, the seller is liable for consequential damages in all cases where he had reason to know of the buyer's general or particular requirements at the time of contracting. It is not necessary that there be a conscious acceptance of an insurer's liability on the seller's part, nor is his obligation for consequential damages limited to cases in which he fails to use due effort in good faith.

Particular needs of the buyer must generally be made known to the seller while general needs must rarely be made known to charge the seller with knowledge.

Any seller who does not wish to take the risk of consequential damages has available the section on contractual limitation of remedy.

4. The burden of proving the extent of loss incurred by way of consequential damage is on the buyer, but the section on liberal administration of remedies rejects any doctrine of certainty which requires almost mathematical precision in the proof of loss. Loss may be determined in any manner which is reasonable under the circumstances. . . .

6. In the case of sale of wares to one in the business of reselling them, resale is one of the requirements of which the seller has reason to know within the meaning of subsection (2)(a).

§ 2–716. Buyer's Right to Specific Performance or Replevin.

(1) Specific performance may be decreed where the goods are unique or in other proper circumstances.

(2) The decree for specific performance may include such terms and conditions as to payment of the price, damages, or other relief as the court may deem just.

(3) The buyer has a right of replevin for goods identified to the contract if after reasonable effort he is unable to effect cover for such goods or the circumstances reasonably indicate that such effort will be unavailing or if the goods have been shipped under reservation and satisfaction of the security interest in them has been made or tendered.

Official Comment

1. The present section continues in general prior policy as to specific performance and injunction against breach. However, without intending to impair in any way the exercise of the court's sound discretion in the matter, this Article seeks to further a more liberal attitude than some courts have shown in connection with the specific performance of contracts of sale.

2. In view of this Article's emphasis on the commercial feasibility of replacement, a new concept of what are "unique" goods is introduced under this section. Specific performance is no longer limited to goods which are already specific or ascertained at the time of contracting. The test of uniqueness under this section must be made in terms of the total situation which characterizes the contract. Output and requirements contracts

involving a particular or peculiarly available source or market present today the typical commercial specific performance situation, as contrasted with contracts for the sale of heirlooms or priceless works of art which were usually involved in the older cases. However, uniqueness is not the sole basis of the remedy under this section for the relief may also be granted "in other proper circumstances" and inability to cover is strong evidence of "other proper circumstances".

3. The legal remedy of replevin is given the buyer in cases in which cover is reasonably unavailable and goods have been identified to the contract. This is in addition to the buyer's right to recover identified goods on the seller's insolvency (Section 2–502).

4. This section is intended to give the buyer rights to the goods comparable to the seller's rights to the price. . . .

§ 2–717. Deduction of Damages From the Price.

The buyer on notifying the seller of his intention to do so may deduct all or any part of the damages resulting from any breach of the contract from any part of the price still due under the same contract.

§ 2–718. Liquidation or Limitation of Damages; Deposits.

(1) Damages for breach by either party may be liquidated in the agreement but only at an amount which is reasonable in the light of the anticipated or actual harm caused by the breach, the difficulties of proof of loss, and the inconvenience or nonfeasibility of otherwise obtaining an adequate remedy. A term fixing unreasonably large liquidated damages is void as a penalty.

(2) Where the seller justifiably withholds delivery of goods because of the buyer's breach, the buyer is entitled to restitution of any amount by which the sum of his payments exceeds

> (a) the amount to which the seller is entitled by virtue of terms liquidating the seller's damages in accordance with subsection (1), or
>
> (b) in the absence of such terms, twenty per cent of the value of the total performance for which the buyer is obligated under the contract or $500, whichever is smaller.

(3) The buyer's right to restitution under subsection (2) is subject to offset to the extent that the seller establishes

> (a) a right to recover damages under the provisions of this Article other than subsection (1), and
>
> (b) the amount or value of any benefits received by the buyer directly or indirectly by reason of the contract.

(4) Where a seller has received payment in goods their reasonable value or the proceeds of their resale shall be treated as payments for the purposes of subsection (2); but if the seller has notice of the buyer's breach before reselling goods received in part performance, his resale is subject to the conditions laid down in this Article on resale by an aggrieved seller (Section 2–706).

Official Comment

1. Under subsection (1) liquidated damage clauses are allowed where the amount involved is reasonable in the light of the circumstances of the case. The subsection sets forth explicitly the elements to be considered in determining the reasonableness of a liquidated damage clause. A term fixing unreasonably large liquidated damages is expressly made void as a penalty. An unreasonably small amount would be subject to similar criticism and might be stricken under the section on unconscionable contracts or clauses.

2. Subsection (2) refuses to recognize a forfeiture unless the amount of the payment so forfeited represents a reasonable liquidation of damages as determined under subsection (1). A special exception is made in the case of small amounts (20% of the price or $500, whichever is smaller) deposited as security. No distinction is made between cases in which the payment is to be applied on the price and those in which it is intended as security for performance. Subsection (2) is applicable to any deposit or down or part payment. In the case of a deposit or turn in of goods resold before the breach, the amount actually received on the resale is to be viewed as the deposit rather than the amount allowed the buyer for the trade in. However, if the seller knows of the breach prior to the resale of the goods turned in, he must make reasonable efforts to realize their true value, and this is assured by requiring him to comply with the conditions laid down in the section on resale by an aggrieved seller.

§ 2–719. Contractual Modification or Limitation of Remedy.

(1) Subject to the provisions of subsections (2) and (3) of this section and of the preceding section on liquidation and limitation of damages,

    (a) the agreement may provide for remedies in addition to or in substitution for those provided in this Article and may limit or alter the measure of damages recoverable under this Article, as by limiting the buyer's remedies to return of the goods and repayment of the price or to repair and replacement of nonconforming goods or parts; and

    (b) resort to a remedy as provided is optional unless the remedy is expressly agreed to be exclusive, in which case it is the sole remedy.

(2) Where circumstances cause an exclusive or limited remedy to fail of its essential purpose, remedy may be had as provided in this Act.

(3) Consequential damages may be limited or excluded unless the limitation or exclusion is unconscionable. Limitation of consequential damages for injury to the person in the case of consumer goods is prima facie unconscionable but limitation of damages where the loss is commercial is not.

Official Comment

1. Under this section parties are left free to shape their remedies to their particular requirements and reasonable agreements limiting or modifying remedies are to be given effect.

However, it is of the very essence of a sales contract that at least minimum adequate remedies be available. If the parties intend to conclude a contract for sale within this Article they must accept the legal consequence that there be at least a fair quantum of remedy for breach of the obligations or duties outlined in the contract. Thus any clause purporting to modify or limit the remedial provisions of this Article in an unconscionable manner is subject to deletion and in that event the remedies made available by this Article are applicable as if the stricken clause had never existed. Similarly, under subsection (2), where an apparently fair and reasonable clause because of circumstances fails in its purpose or operates to deprive either party of the substantial value of the bargain, it must give way to the general remedy provisions of this Article.

2. Subsection (1)(b) creates a presumption that clauses prescribing remedies are cumulative rather than exclusive. If the parties intend the term to describe the sole remedy under the contract, this must be clearly expressed.

3. Subsection (3) recognizes the validity of clauses limiting or excluding consequential damages but makes it clear that they may not operate in an unconscionable manner. Actually such terms are merely an allocation of unknown or undeterminable risks. The seller in all cases is free to disclaim warranties in the manner provided in Section 2–316.

§ 2–721. Remedies for Fraud.

Remedies for material misrepresentation or fraud include all remedies available under this Article for non-fraudulent breach. Neither rescission or a claim for rescission of the contract for sale nor rejection or return of the goods shall bar or be deemed inconsistent with a claim for damages or other remedy.

§ 2–723. Proof of Market Price: Time and Place.

(1) If an action based on anticipatory repudiation comes to trial before the time for performance with respect to some or all of the goods, any damages based on market price (Section 2–708 or Section 2–713) shall be determined according to the price of such goods prevailing at the time when the aggrieved party learned of the repudiation.

(2) If evidence of a price prevailing at the times or places described in this Article is not readily available the price prevailing within any reasonable time before or after the time described or at any other place which in commercial judgment or under usage of trade would serve as a reasonable substitute for the one described may be used, making any proper allowance for the cost of transporting the goods to or from such other place.

(3) Evidence of a relevant price prevailing at a time or place other than the one described in this Article offered by one party is not admissible

unless and until he has given the other party such notice as the court finds sufficient to prevent unfair surprise.

§ 2–725. Statute of Limitations in Contracts for Sale.

(1) An action for breach of any contract for sale must be commenced within four years after the cause of action has accrued. By the original agreement the parties may reduce the period of limitation to not less than one year but may not extend it.

(2) A cause of action accrues when the breach occurs, regardless of the aggrieved party's lack of knowledge of the breach. A breach of warranty occurs when tender of delivery is made, except that where a warranty explicitly extends to future performance of the goods and discovery of the breach must await the time of such performance the cause of action accrues when the breach is or should have been discovered.

(3) Where an action commenced within the time limited by subsection (1) is so terminated as to leave available a remedy by another action for the same breach such other action may be commenced after the expiration of the time limited and within six months after the termination of the first action unless the termination resulted from voluntary discontinuance or from dismissal for failure or neglect to prosecute.

(4) This section does not alter the law on tolling of the statute of limitations nor does it apply to causes of action which have accrued before this Act becomes effective.

REVISION OF UNIFORM COMMERCIAL CODE
ARTICLE 2—SALES *

Extracts From July 1997 Draft

Table of Contents

PART 1. GENERAL PROVISIONS

PART 2. FORMATION, TERMS, AND READJUSTMENT
OF CONTRACT

PART 3. GENERAL OBLIGATION AND
CONSTRUCTION OF CONTRACT

PART 4. WARRANTIES

73

REVISION OF UNIFORM COMMERCIAL CODE
ARTICLE 2—SALES

PART 1

GENERAL PROVISIONS

§ 2–101. Short Title.

This article may be cited as Uniform Commercial Code—Sales.

§ 2–102. Definitions.

(a) Unless the context otherwise requires, in this article:

(1) "Authenticate" means to sign, or to execute or adopt a symbol, or encrypt a record in whole or in part with present intent to identify the authenticating party, or to adopt or accept a record or term, or to establish the authenticity of a record or term that contains the authentication or to which a record containing the authentication refers.

(2) "Between merchants", with respect to a transaction, means between parties both of which are chargeable with the knowledge or skill of merchants. . . .

(5) "Commercial unit" means a unit of goods which by commercial usage is a single whole for purposes of sale and whose division materially impairs its character or value in the relevant market or in use. A commercial unit may be a single article, such as a machine; a set of articles, such as a suite of furniture or a line of machinery; a quantity, such as a gross or carload; or any other unit treated in use or in the relevant market as a single whole.

(6) "Conforming" goods or performance under a contract for sale means goods or performance that are in accordance with the obligations under the contract.

(7) "Conspicuous" means so displayed or presented that a reasonable person against whom it operates ought to have noticed it or, in the case of an electronic message intended to evoke a response without the need for review by an individual, in a form that would enable a reasonably configured electronic agent to take it into account or react to it without review of the message by an individual.

(8) "Consumer" means an individual who buys or contracts to buy goods that, at the time of contracting, are intended by the individual to be used primarily for personal, family, or household use. The term does not include an individual who buys or contracts to buy goods that, at the time of contracting, are intended by the individual to be used primarily for professional or commercial purposes. . . .

(10) "Contract for sale" means a present sale or a contract to sell at a future date, whether or not the goods are future goods....

(12) "Electronic agent" means a computer program or other automated means used, selected, or programmed by a party to initiate or respond to electronic messages or performances in whole or in part without review by an individual.

(13) "Electronic" means electrical, digital, magnetic, optical, electromagnetic, or any other form of wave propagation, or by any other technology that entails capabilities similar to those technologies.

(14) "Electronic message" means a record that, for purposes of communication to another person, is stored, generated, or transmitted by electronic, optical, or similar means. The term includes electronic data interchange, electronic or voice mail, facsimile, telex, telecopying, scanning, and similar communications.

(15) "Electronic transaction" means a transaction formed by electronic messages in which the messages of one or both parties will not be reviewed by an individual as a routine step in forming the contract....

(18) "Future goods" means goods that at the time of contracting are neither existing nor identified.

(19) "Good faith" means honesty in fact and the observance of reasonable commercial standards of fair dealing.

(20) "Goods" means all things, including specially manufactured goods, that are movable at the time of identification to a contract for sale or, unless the context otherwise requires, future goods. The term includes the unborn young of animals, growing crops, and other identified things attached to realty in Section 2–108. The term does not include money in which the price is to be paid, the subject of foreign exchange transactions, documents, letters of credit, information, instruments, investment property, accounts, chattel paper, deposit accounts, general intangibles, and payment intangibles....

(22) "Lot" means a parcel or single article that is the subject matter of a separate sale or delivery, whether or not it is sufficient to perform the contract.

(23) "Merchant" means a person that deals in goods of the kind involved in the transaction, a person that by occupation purports to have knowledge or skill peculiar to the practices or goods involved in the transaction, or a person to which knowledge or skill may be attributed by the person's employment of an agent or broker or other intermediary that purports to have the knowledge or skill.

(24) "Present sale" means a sale that is accomplished by the making of a contract.

(25) "Receipt":

    (A) with respect to goods, means taking delivery; and

    (B) with respect to an electronic record, means when it enters an information processing system in a form capable of being processed by a system of that type and the recipient uses or has designated that system for the purpose of receiving records or information. "Receive" has an analogous meaning.

(26) "Record" means information that is inscribed on a tangible medium, or that is stored in an electronic or other medium and is retrievable in perceivable form....

(b) Other definitions applying to this Article and the sections in which they appear are:

"Acceptance of goods." Section 2–706....

"Assignment." Section 2–503(a)....

"Breach of contract." Sections 2–701(a), 2–815(a).

"Consequential damages." Section 2–806.

"Cover." Section 2–825(a).

"Delegation." Section 2–503(b)....

"Incidental damages." Section 2–805.

"Identification." Section 2–502....

"Installment contract." Section 2–710(a).

"Repudiation." Section 2–712(b)....

"Substantial impairment." Section 2–701(c).

"Waiver." Sections 2–210, 2–702....

(c) In addition, Article 1 contains general definitions and principles of construction that apply throughout this article.

§ 2–103. Scope.

(a) This article applies to transactions in goods.

(b) If a transaction involves both information and goods, this article applies to the aspects of the transaction which involve the goods and their performance and rights in the goods other than the physical medium containing the information, its packaging, and its documentation. However, this article applies to a sale of a computer program that was not developed specifically for a particular transaction and that is embedded in goods other than a copy of the program or an information processing machine, if the program was not the subject of a separate license with the buyer.

(c) Except as otherwise provided in subsection (b), to the extent that another article of this [Act] applies to a transaction in goods, this article does not apply to the part of the transaction governed by the other article.

(d) This article does not apply to a foreign exchange transaction.

§ 2–105. Unconscionable Contract or Term.

(a) If a court finds as a matter of law that a contract or a term of the contract was unconscionable at the time the contract was made or was induced by unconscionable conduct, the court may refuse to enforce the contract, enforce the remainder of the contract without the term, or so limit the application of the term to avoid an unconscionable result.

(b) Before making a finding of unconscionability under subsection (a), the court, on motion of a party or its own motion, shall afford the parties a reasonable opportunity to present evidence as to the setting, purpose, and effect of the contract or term thereof or of the conduct.

§ 2–106. Interest and Part Interest in Goods.

(a) Goods must be both existing and identified before an interest in them may be transferred.

(b) A part interest in existing, identified goods may be sold.

(c) A purported present sale of future goods or an interest in future goods is a contract to sell future goods.

(d) An undivided share in a described bulk of fungible goods is sufficiently identified to be sold, even if the quantity of the bulk is not determined. Any proportion of the bulk or quantity agreed upon by number, weight, or other measure, to the extent of the seller's interest in the bulk, may be sold to the buyer. The buyer is an owner in common.

§ 2–107. Goods to Be Severed From Real Property; Recording.

(a) A contract for the sale of minerals, oil, gas, or similar things to be extracted, or a structure or its materials to be removed, from real property, is a contract for the sale of goods if they are to be severed by the seller. Until severance, a purported present sale of those things, other than a sale that is effective as a transfer of an interest in the real property, is only a contract to sell future goods.

(b) A contract for the sale, apart from an interest in real property, of growing crops, timber to be cut, or other things attached to real property and capable of severance without material harm to the real property other than the things described in subsection (a), is a contract for the sale of goods, whether the thing is to be severed by the buyer or seller and even if it forms part of the real property at the time of contracting. The parties may effect a present sale before severance by identification of the goods.

(c) The rights of a buyer and seller under this section are subject to rights of third parties under the laws relating to records of real property. A contract for sale may be executed and recorded as a document transferring an interest in real property. The recording constitutes notice to third parties of the buyer's rights under the contract for sale.

§ 2–108. Effect of Agreement.

(a) Except as otherwise provided in Section 1–102 and this article, the effect of any provision may be varied by agreement.

(b) The absence of a phrase such as "unless otherwise agreed" does not by itself preclude the parties from varying the provision by agreement.

77

(c) Whenever this article allocates a risk or imposes a burden as between the parties, an agreement may shift the allocation and apportion the risk or burden.

PART 2

FORMATION, TERMS, AND READJUSTMENT OF CONTRACT

§ 2–201. Formal Requirements.

(a) Except as otherwise provided in this section, a claim for breach of contract for sale in the price of $10,000 or more is not enforceable by way of action or defense against a person that denies that an agreement was made, unless there is a record authenticated by the person against which the claim is asserted as the record of that person and which is sufficient to indicate that a contract was made. A record is not insufficient merely because it omits or incorrectly states a term, including a quantity term. If the record contains a quantity term, the claim is not enforceable beyond that quantity.

(b) If an authenticated record in confirmation of a contract is sufficient against the sender and is sent within a reasonable time to the other party, the record is sufficient against the other party who is a merchant, unless the merchant sends a notice of objection to the record within 10 days after the record is received.

(c) A claim for breach of an otherwise valid contract which is barred under subsection (a) is enforceable if:

(1) the goods are to be specially manufactured or processed for the buyer, the seller substantially manufactures or processes or makes commitments for the procurement of the goods in performance of a contract believed in good faith to exist, and the seller cannot resell the goods at a reasonable price;

(2) the conduct of both parties in performing the agreement recognizes that a contract was formed;

(3) reliance by one party on representations or an agreement under law outside of this [Act] estops the other party from raising the lack of a sufficient authenticated record as a defense; or

(4) the party against whom enforcement is sought, in pleading or testimony in court or otherwise under oath, admits facts from which a contract for sale can be found.

(d) A claim for breach of contract enforceable under this section is not unenforceable on the ground that it is not capable of being performed within one year or any other applicable period after its making.

§ 2–202. Parol or Extrinsic Evidence.

Terms on which confirmatory records of the parties agree, or which are otherwise set forth in a record intended by the parties as a final expression of their agreement with respect to the included terms, may not be contradicted by evidence of a previous agreement or contemporaneous oral agreement. However, terms in a record may be explained by any relevant evidence and may be supplemented by evidence of:

    (1) course of performance, usage of trade, or course of dealing; and

    (2) noncontradictory additional terms unless:

        (A) The terms if agreed upon by the parties would certainly have been included in the record; or

        (B) The court finds that the record was intended as a complete and exclusive statement of the terms of the agreement.

§ 2–203. Formation in General.

(a) A contract may be made in any manner sufficient to show agreement, including by offer and acceptance or conduct of both parties which recognizes the existence of a contract.

(b) A contract may be found if the parties intend to form a contract, even if the time that the agreement was made cannot be determined, one or more terms are left open or to be agreed upon, the records of the parties do not otherwise establish a contract, or one party reserves the right to modify terms.

(c) Even if one or more terms are left open, a contract does not fail for indefiniteness if the parties intended to form a contract and there is a reasonably certain basis for an appropriate remedy.

(d) Conspicuous language in a record which expressly conditions the intention of the proposing party to contract only upon agreement by the other party to terms proposed in the record is effective to prevent contract formation.

§ 2–204. Firm Offers; Sealed Records.

(a) An offer by a merchant to enter into a contract made in an authenticated record that by its terms gives assurance that the offer will be held open is not revocable for lack of consideration during the time stated. If a time is not stated, the offer is irrevocable for a reasonable time not exceeding 90 days. A term of assurance in a record supplied by the offeree to the offeror is ineffective unless the term is conspicuous.

(b) Affixing a seal to a record evidencing a contract for sale or an offer does not make the record a sealed instrument. The law with respect to sealed instruments does not apply to the contract or offer.

§ 2–205. Offer and Acceptance.

(a) Unless otherwise unambiguously indicated by the language or circumstances, the following rules apply:

(1) An offer to make a contract invites acceptance in any manner and by any medium reasonable under the circumstances. Subject to Section 2–203(d), a definite expression of acceptance in a record that also contains terms varying from the offer is an acceptance.

(2) An order or other offer to buy or acquire goods for prompt or current shipment invites acceptance by a prompt promise to ship or by a prompt or current shipment of goods. If the order or offer is construed to invite acceptance by the shipment of non-conforming goods, the non-conforming shipment is not an acceptance if the seller seasonably notifies the buyer that the shipment is offered only as an accommodation.

(b) If the beginning of a requested performance is a reasonable mode of acceptance, an offeror that is not notified of acceptance within a reasonable time may treat the offer as having lapsed before acceptance.

§ 2–206. Consumer Contracts; Records.

(a) In a consumer contract, if a consumer agrees to a record, any nonnegotiated term that a reasonable consumer in a transaction of this type would not reasonably expect to be in the record is excluded from the contract, unless the consumer had knowledge of the term before agreeing to the record.

(b) Before deciding whether to exclude a term under subsection (a), the court, on motion of a party or its own motion, after affording the parties a reasonable and expeditious opportunity to present evidence on whether the term should be included or excluded from the contract, shall decide whether the contract should be interpreted to exclude the term.

(c) This section shall not operate to exclude an otherwise enforceable term disclaiming or modifying an implied warranty.

§ 2–207. Effect of Varying Terms in Records.

(a) This section is subject to Sections 2–202 and 2–206.

(b) If a contract is formed by offer and acceptance and the acceptance is by a record containing terms varying from the offer or by conduct of the parties that recognizes the existence of a contract but the records of the parties do not otherwise establish a contract for sale, the contract includes:

(1) terms in the records of the parties to the extent that the records agree;

(2) terms not in records to which the parties have agreed;

(3) terms supplied or incorporated under any provision of this [Act]; and

(4) terms in a record supplied by a party to which the other party has expressly agreed.

(c) if a contract is formed by any manner permitted under this article and either party or both parties confirms the agreement by a record, the contract includes:

(1) terms agreed to prior to the confirmation;

(2) terms in a confirming record that do not materially vary the prior agreement and are not seasonably objected to;

(3) terms in confirming records to the extent that they agree; and

(4) terms supplied or incorporated under any provision of this [Act].

§ 2–208. Course of Performance or Practical Construction.

(a) A "course of performance" is a sequence of conduct between the parties to a particular transaction that exists if:

(1) the agreement of the parties with respect to the transaction involves repeated occasions for performance by a party;

(2) that party performs on one or more occasions; and

(3) the other party, with knowledge of the nature of the performance and opportunity for objection to it, accepts the performance or acquiesces in it without objection.

(b) A course of performance between the parties is relevant to ascertaining the meaning of the parties' agreement, may give particular meaning to specific terms of the agreement, and may supplement or qualify the terms of the agreement.

(c) Except as otherwise provided in subsection (d), the express terms of an agreement and any applicable course of performance, course of dealing, or usage of trade must be construed whenever reasonable as consistent with each other. If such construction is unreasonable:

(1) express terms prevail over course of performance, course of dealing, and usage of trade;

(2) course of performance prevails over course of dealing and usage of trade; and

(3) course of dealing prevails over usage of trade.

(d) Subject to Section 2–210, course of performance is relevant to show a waiver or modification of a term inconsistent with the course of performance.

§ 2–209. Modification, Rescission, and Waiver.

(a) An agreement made in good faith which modifies a contract under this article is binding without consideration.

(b) Except in a consumer contract, a contract that contains a term that excludes modification or rescission except by an authenticated record may not be otherwise modified or rescinded. However, a party whose language or conduct is inconsistent with the term requiring an authenticated record may not assert that term if the language or conduct induced the other party to change its position reasonably and in good faith.

(c) Subject to subsection (b), a term in a contract may be waived by the party for whose benefit it was included. Language, conduct or a course of performance between the parties may be relevant to show a waiver. The waiver of an executory portion of a contract, however, may be retracted by seasonable notification received by the other party that strict performance is required of any term waived unless the waiver induced the other party to change its position reasonably and in good faith.

§ 2–213. Electronic Transactions and Messages: Timing of Contract and Effectiveness of Message.

(a) If an electronic message initiated by a party or an electronic agent evokes an electronic response and the messages reflect an intent to be bound, a contract exists when:

(1) the response signifying acceptance is received; or

(2) if the response consists of electronically furnishing the requested information or notice of access to the information, when the information or notice is received unless the originating message prohibited that form of response.

(b) Subject to Section 2–211, an electronic message is effective when received, even if no individual is aware of its receipt.

(c) Subject to subsection (d), operations of one or more electronic agents which confirm the existence of an agreement are effective to form an agreement even if no individual representing either party was aware of or reviewed the action or its results.

(d) In an electronic transaction, the following rules apply:

(1) An agreement is formed by the interaction of two electronic agents if the interaction results in both agents each engaging in operations that signify agreement, such as by engaging in performing the agreement, ordering or instructing performance, accepting performance, or making a record of the existence of an agreement.

(2) An agreement may be formed by the interaction of an electronic agent and an individual. An agreement is formed if an individual has reason to know that the individual is dealing with an electronic agent and performs actions the person should know will cause the agent to perform or to permit further use, or that are clearly indicated as constituting acceptance regardless of other contemporaneous expressions by the individual to which the electronic agent cannot react.

(3) The terms of the contract include terms on which the parties have previously agreed, terms which the electronic agents could take into account, and, terms provided by this article or other law.

PART 3

GENERAL OBLIGATION AND CONSTRUCTION OF CONTRACT

§ 2–302. Performance at Single Time.

(a) If all of a seller's performance can be rendered at one time, the performance is due at one time and the buyer's reciprocal performance is due only on tender of full performance.

(b) If circumstances give either party the right to make or demand performance in parts or over a period of time, payment, if it can be apportioned, may be demanded for each part performance.

(c) If payment cannot be apportioned or the agreement or the circumstances indicate that payment may not be demanded for part performance, payment is due on completion of full performance.

§ 2–303. Open–Price Term.

(a) The parties, if they so intend, may form a contract for sale even if the price is:

(1) not agreed to;

(2) left to be agreed by the parties and they fail to agree; or

(3) to be fixed in terms of some agreed market or other standard as set or recorded by a third party or agency and it is not so set or recorded.

(b) If a contract formed under subsection (a), the price is a reasonable price at the time that the seller is required by the contract to make delivery.

(c) A price to be fixed by the seller or the buyer must be fixed in good faith.

(d) If a price left to be fixed otherwise than by agreement of the parties fails to be fixed through fault of one party, the other party at that party's option may treat the contract as canceled or may fix a reasonable price.

(e) If the parties intend not to be bound unless the contract price is fixed or agreed to and it is not fixed or agreed to, a contract is not formed. In that case, the buyer shall return any goods already received or, if unable to do so, pay their reasonable value at the time of transfer, and the seller shall return any portion of the contract price paid on account.

§ 2–304. Output, Requirements, and Exclusive Dealing.

(a) A contractual term that measures the quantity of goods by the output of the seller or the requirements of the buyer means the actual output or requirements that may occur in good faith. A party may not offer or demand a quantity unreasonably disproportionate to a stated estimate or, in the absence of a stated estimate, to any normal or otherwise comparable previous output or requirements unless there are no outputs or requirements in good faith.

(b) An agreement for exclusive dealing in the kind of goods concerned imposes an obligation by the seller to use best efforts to supply the goods and by the buyer to use best efforts to promote their sale.

§ 2–306. Time for Performance Not Specified.

(a) Except as otherwise expressly provided in this article, the time for performance or any other action under an agreement in which a time for performance is not specified is a reasonable time.

(b) If an agreement provides for successive performances but is indefinite in duration, the duration of the agreement is a reasonable time. Subject to Section 2–311, either party may terminate the contract at any time.

§ 2–307. Options and Cooperation Respecting Performance.

(a) An agreement that is otherwise sufficiently definite to be a contract is enforceable even if it leaves particulars of performance open, to be specified by one of the parties, or to be fixed by agreement.

(b) If one party is required to specify the particulars of performance, the specification must be made in good faith and within limits of commercial reasonableness.

(c) An agreement providing that the performance of the seller be to the satisfaction of the buyer without further specifying the standard of performance requires that the performance be such that a reasonable person in the position of the buyer would be satisfied.

(d) A specification relating to an assortment of goods is at the buyer's option. Except as otherwise provided in subsection (e), a specification or arrangement relating to shipment is at the seller's option.

(e) If a specification by one party would materially affect the other party's performance but is not seasonably made or one party's cooperation is necessary to the agreed performance of the other but is not seasonably forthcoming, the other party, in addition to all other remedies:

> (1) is excused for any resulting delay in the party's own performance; and

> (2) may proceed to perform in any reasonable manner or, after the time for a material part of the party's own performance, treat the failure to specify or cooperate as a breach of contract.

§ 2–310. Termination; Survival of Obligations and Terms.

(a) Except as otherwise provided in subsection (b), on termination of a contract, all obligations that are still executory on both sides are discharged.

(b) The following survive termination of a contract:

> (1) a right based on a previous breach or performance of the contract;

> (2) a term limiting the scope, manner, method, or location of the exercise of rights in the goods;

> (3) an obligation of confidentiality, nondisclosure, or noncompetition;

> (4) an obligation to return or dispose of goods;

> (5) a choice of law or forum;

> (6) an obligation to arbitrate or otherwise resolve disputes through alternative dispute resolution procedures;

> (7) a term limiting the time for commencing an action or for providing notice;

(8) an indemnity term;

(9) a limitation of remedy or modification or disclaimer of warranty;

(10) any term limiting disclosure of information; and

(11) other rights, remedies, or limitations if in the circumstances such survival is necessary to achieve the purposes of the parties.

(c) The obligation under subsection (b)(3) must be promptly performed.

§ 2–311. Termination; Notification.

(a) A party may not terminate a contract, except on the happening of an agreed event, such as the expiration of the stated term, unless the other party receives notice of the termination and is given a reasonable time before the termination is effective.

(b) A term dispensing with notification is invalid if its operation is unconscionable. However, a term specifying standards for the nature and timing of notification is enforceable if the standards are not manifestly unreasonable.

§ 2–312. Sale by Auction.

(a) In a sale by auction, if goods are put up in lots, each lot is the subject of a separate sale.

(b) A sale by auction is complete when the auctioneer so announces by the fall of the hammer or in any other customary manner. If a bid is made during the process of completing the sale but before a prior bid is accepted, the auctioneer may in its discretion reopen the bidding or declare the goods sold under the prior bid.

(c) A sale by auction is subject to the seller's power to withdraw the goods unless at the time the goods are put up or during the course of the auction it is announced in express terms that the power to withdraw the goods is not reserved. In an auction where power to withdraw the goods is reserved, the auctioneer may withdraw the goods at any time until completion of the sale is announced. In an auction where power to withdraw the goods is not reserved, after the auctioneer calls for bids on an article or lot, the article or lot may not be withdrawn unless no bid is made within a reasonable time. In either case, a bidder may retract a bid until the auctioneer's announcement of completion of the sale, but a bidder's retraction does not revive any previous bid. . . .

PART 4

WARRANTIES

§ 2–401. Definitions.

In this part:

(1) "Damage" means all loss resulting in the ordinary course from a breach of warranty, including injury to a person or property as permitted in Section 2–806.

(2) "Goods" includes a component incorporated in substantially the same condition into other goods.

(3) "Immediate buyer" means a buyer in a contractual relationship with the seller.

(4) "Remote buyer" means a buyer or lessee from a person other than the seller against which a claim for breach of warranty breach is asserted.

(5) "Representation" means a description, demonstration or depiction of the goods, an affirmation of fact relating to the goods, or a sample or model of the goods.

(6) "Seller" includes an auctioneer or liquidator that fails to disclose that it is acting on behalf of a principal.

§ 2–402. Warranty of Title and Against Infringement; Buyer's Obligation Against Infringement.

(a) A seller in a contract for sale warrants that:

(1) the title conveyed is good and its transfer is rightful and does not, because of any colorable claim to or interest in the goods, unreasonably expose the buyer to litigation; and

(2) the goods will be received free from any security interest or other lien or encumbrance of which the buyer at the time of contracting does not have knowledge.

(b) A warranty under subsection (a) may be disclaimed or modified only by express language or by circumstances giving the immediate buyer reason to know that the seller does not claim title or purports to sell only such right or title as the seller or a third party may have. In an electronic transaction that does not involve review of the record by an individual, language is sufficient if it is conspicuous and related to the warranty of title against infringement. Otherwise, language in a record is sufficient to disclaim warranties under this section if it is conspicuous and states "There is no warranty of title or against infringement in this sale" or words of similar import.

(c) A seller who is a merchant that regularly deals in goods of the kind sold warrants that the goods will be delivered free of the rightful claim of a third party by way of infringement or the like. However, a buyer that furnishes specifications to the seller holds the seller harmless against any claim of infringement or the like that arises out of compliance with the specifications.

(d) A seller's warranty under this section, made to an immediate buyer, extends to any remote buyer or transferee that may reasonably be expected to buy the goods and that suffers damage from breach of the warranty. The rights and remedies of a remote buyer or transferee against the seller for breach of warranty are determined by the terms of the contract between the seller and the immediate buyer.

(e) A right of action for breach of warranty under this section accrues under Section 2–814(b) when the buyer or transferee discovers or should have discovered the breach.

§ 2–403. Express Warranty to Immediate Buyer.

(a) If a seller makes a representation or promise relating to the goods to an immediate buyer, the representation or the promise becomes part of the agreement unless a reasonable person in the position of the immediate buyer would not believe that the representation or promise became part of the agreement or would believe that the representation was merely of the value of the goods or purported to be merely the seller's opinion or commendation of the goods. An obligation may be created under this section even though the seller does not use formal words, such as "warranty" or "guarantee."

(b) A representation or a promise that becomes part of the agreement is an express warranty and the seller has an obligation to the immediate buyer that the goods will conform to the representation or, if a sample is involved, that the whole of the goods will conform to the sample, or that the promise will be performed. The obligation is breached if the goods do not conform to any representation at the time when the tender of delivery was completed or if the promise was not performed when due.

(c) A seller's obligation under this section may be created by representations and promises made in a medium for communication to the public, including advertising, if the immediate buyer had knowledge of them at the time of the agreement.

§ 2–404. Implied Warranty of Merchantability; Usage of Trade.

(a) Subject to Sections 2–406 and 2–407, a seller that is a merchant with respect to goods of that kind makes in a contract for sale an implied warranty that the goods are merchantable. The serving for value of food or drink to be consumed on the premises or elsewhere is a sale under this section.

(b) To be merchantable, goods, at a minimum, must:

(1) pass without objection in the trade under the agreed description;

(2) in the case of fungible goods, be of fair, average quality within the description;

(3) be fit for the ordinary purposes for which goods of that description are used;

(4) run, within the variations permitted by the agreement, of even kind, quality, and quantity within each unit and among all units involved;

(5) be adequately contained, packaged, and labeled as the agreement or circumstances may require; and

(6) conform to the promise or affirmations of fact made on the container or label.

(c) Subject to Section 2–408, implied warranties other than those described in this section may arise from course of dealing or usage of trade.

§ 2–405. Implied Warranty of Fitness for Particular Purpose.

Subject to Sections 2–406 and 2–407, if a seller at the time of contracting has reason to know any particular purpose for which the goods are required and that the buyer is relying on the seller's skill or judgment to select or furnish suitable goods, there is an implied warranty that the goods are fit for that purpose.

§ 2–406. Disclaimer or Modification of Warranty.

(a) Language or conduct relevant to the creation of an express warranty and language or conduct tending to disclaim or modify an express warranty must be construed wherever reasonable as consistent with each other. Subject to Section 2–202 with regard to parol or extrinsic evidence, language or conduct disclaiming or modifying an express warranty is ineffective to the extent that this construction is unreasonable.

(b) Except as otherwise provided in Section 2–402(b) and (e), an implied warranty is disclaimed or modified by language or an expression that, under the circumstances, makes it clear that the implied warranty has been disclaimed or modified. An implied warranty may also be disclaimed or modified by course of performance, course of dealing, or usage of trade.

(c) Except as otherwise provided in subsection (e), language in a record is sufficient to disclaim or modify an implied warranty if the language is conspicuous and:

   (1) in the case of the implied warranty of merchantability, mentions merchantability;

   (2) in the case of the implied warranty of fitness, states that "the goods are not warranted to be fit for any particular purpose", or words of similar import;

   (3) Unless the circumstances indicate otherwise, states that the goods are sold "as is" or "with all faults" or words of similar import.

(d) If, before entering into a contract, a buyer has examined the goods, sample, or model as fully as desired or has declined to examine them, there is no implied warranty with regard to conditions that an examination in the circumstances would have revealed to the buyer.

(e) Except in a sale by auction under Section 2–312, language in a consumer contract is sufficient to disclaim or modify an implied warranty only if:

   (1) At the time of contracting, a seller in good faith passes through to a buyer an express warranty obligation created by another seller under Section 2–408(b) that is reasonable in scope, duration and remedies and there is conspicuous language in a record stating, for example, "You are receiving an express warranty obligation from the

[manufacturer] instead of any implied warranty of merchantability or fitness from us;'' or

(2) Conspicuous language in a record which language the consumer has separately authenticated states: "Unless we say otherwise in the contract, we make no promises about the quality or usefulness of what you are buying. They may not work. They may not be fit for any specific purpose that you may have in mind."

(f) Remedies for breach of warranty may be limited in accordance with this article with respect to liquidation or limitation of damages and contractual modification of remedy.

§ 2–407. Cumulation and Conflict of Warranties.

Warranties, whether express or implied, must be construed as consistent with each other and as cumulative. However, if that construction is unreasonable, the intent of the parties determines which warranty prevails. In ascertaining that intent, the following rules apply:

(1) Exact or technical specifications prevail over an inconsistent sample or model or general language of description.

(2) A sample, model or demonstration prevails over inconsistent general language of description.

(3) Except in a consumer contract, an express warranty prevails over an inconsistent implied warranty other than an implied warranty of fitness for a particular purpose.

§ 2–408. Extension of Express Warranty to Remote Buyer and Transferee.

(a) In this section, "goods" means new goods and goods that are sold as new goods.

(b) If a seller makes a representation or a promise relating to goods on or in a container, on a label, in a record, or that is packaged with or otherwise accompanies the goods and authorizes another person to deliver the container, label, or record to a remote buyer and it is so delivered, the seller has an obligation to the remote buyer and its transferee, and in the case of a remote consumer buyer, to any member of the family or household of the remote consumer buyer, that the goods will conform to the representation or that the promise will be performed, unless a reasonable person in the position of the remote buyer would not believe the representation or promise or would believe that any representation was merely of the value of the goods or purported to be merely the seller's opinion or commendation of the goods.

(c) If a seller makes a representation or a promise relating to the goods in a medium for communication to the public, including advertising, and a remote buyer with knowledge of the representation or promise buys or leases the goods from a person the seller has an obligation to the remote buyer and its transferee and, in the case of a remote consumer to buyer, to any member of the family or household of that consumer buyer, that the goods will conform to the representation, or that the promise will be performed, unless a reasonable person in the position of the remote buyer would not believe the representation or promise or would believe that the representation was merely of the value of the goods or purported to be merely the seller's opinion or commendation of the goods.

(d) An obligation may be created under this section even though the seller does not use formal words, such as "warranty" or "guaranty".

(e) An obligation arising under this section is breached when the goods are received by the remote buyer if the goods, at the time they left the seller's control, did not conform to any representation made, or if the promise is not performed when due.

(f) The following rules apply to the remedies for breach of an obligation created under this section:

(1) A seller under subsections (b) and (c) may modify or limit the remedies available to a remote buyer for breach, but a modification or limitation is not effective unless it is communicated to the remote buyer with the representation or promise.

(2) Damages may be proved in any manner that is reasonable. Unless special circumstances show proximate damages of a different amount;

(A) a measure of damages if the goods do not conform to a representation is the value of the goods as represented less the value of the goods as delivered; and

(B) a measure of damages for breach of a promise is the value of the promised performance less the value of any performance made.

(3) A seller in breach under this section is liable for incidental or consequential damages under Sections 2–805 and 2–806 but is not liable for consequential damages for a remote buyer's lost profits;

[(4) A remote consumer buyer that bought the goods on credit and is entitled to damages under subsection (f)(2) may, upon notifying the immediate seller, deduct damages from any part of the price still due.]

(5) An action for breach of an obligation under subsection (e) is timely if commenced within the time provided in Section 2–814.

(g) This section is subject to Section 2–409(b).

§ 2–409. Extension of Express or Implied Warranty.

(a) A seller's express warranty under Section 2–403 or implied warranty under Section 2–405 or 2–406 made to an immediate buyer extends to any buyer or transferee, and in the case of a consumer buyer, to any member of the family or household of the buyer, that may reasonably be expected to use or be affected by the goods and that is damaged by a breach of warranty. The rights and remedies of the buyer, members of a consumer buyer's family or household or a transferee against the seller for breach of a warranty extended under this subsection are determined by the terms of the contract between the seller and the immediate buyer. However, the seller is not liable for consequential lost profits for breach of warranty under this section.

(b) This section and Sections 2–402 and 2–408 do not:

(1) diminish the rights and remedies of a third party beneficiary or assignee under the law of contracts or of persons to which goods are transferred by operation of law;

(2) displace principles of law and equity that extend an express or implied warranty to or for the benefit of a remote buyer, transferee, or other person.

(c) The operation of this section may not be excluded, modified, or limited unless the seller has a substantial interest based on the nature of the goods in having a warranty extend only to the immediate buyer.

PART 5

TRANSFERS, IDENTIFICATION, CREDITORS, AND GOOD–FAITH PURCHASERS

§ 2–502. Insurable Interest in Goods; Manner of Identification of Goods.

(a) Identification of goods as goods to which a contract refers may be made at any time and in any manner expressly agreed to by the parties. In the absence of express agreement, identification occurs when:

(1) the contract is made, if the contract is for the sale of existing and described goods;

(2) goods are shipped, marked, or otherwise designated by the seller as goods to which the contract refers, if the contract is for the sale of future goods other than those described in paragraph (3) or (4);

(3) crops are planted or otherwise become growing crops, if the contract is for the sale of crops to be harvested within 12 months or the next normal harvest season after contracting, whichever is longer; or

(4) young are conceived, if the contract is for the sale of the unborn young of animals to be born within 12 months after contracting.

(b) A buyer obtains a special property interest and an insurable interest in existing goods identified to the contract, even if the goods are nonconforming and the buyer has an option to return or reject them.

(c) A seller has an insurable interest in identified goods as long as title to or a security interest in the goods is retained. If the identification is by the seller alone, the seller may substitute other goods for those identified until breach of contract or insolvency or notification to the buyer that the identification is final.

(d) This section does not impair an insurable interest recognized as such under any other law.

§ 2–503. Assignment of Rights; Delegation of Duties.

(a) All rights of a seller or buyer, including a right to damages for breach of the whole contract or a right arising out of the assignor's due performance of its entire obligation, may be assigned unless the assignment would materially change the duty of the other party, increase the burden or risk imposed on that party by the contract, or impair that party's likelihood of obtaining return performance.

(b) A party may delegate to another person its performance under a contract for sale unless the other party to the contract has a substantial interest in having the original promisor perform or directly control the performance required by the contract. A delegation of performance does not relieve the delegating party of any duty to perform or liability for breach.

(c) Acceptance of a delegation of duties by an assignee constitutes a promise by the assignee to perform those duties. The promise is enforceable by the assignor or the other party to the original contract. The other party may treat any assignment or transfer that delegates performance as creating reasonable grounds for insecurity and, without prejudice to the party's rights against the assignor, may demand assurance of due performance from the assignee.

(d) An assignment or transfer of "the contract" or "all my rights under the contract", or an assignment or transfer in similar general terms, is an assignment of rights. Unless the language or the circumstances indicate the contrary, as in an assignment for security, the assignment or transfer is a delegation of performance of the duties of the assignor.

(e) Subject to Article 9, if a contractual term prohibits the assignment of rights otherwise assignable under subsection (a), the assignment is effective. However, whether or not the contract so provides, the assignment is a breach of contract for which damages under this article are available.

(f) A contractual term prohibiting the delegation of duties otherwise delegable under subsection (c) is enforceable, and an attempted delegation is not effective. A prohibition of assignment or transfer of "the contract" must be construed as precluding only the delegation to the assignee or transferee of the assignor's duty to perform.

PART 6

PERFORMANCE

§ 2–601. General Obligations.

Parties are obligated to perform in accordance with the contract.

§ 2–602. Manner of Seller's Tender of Delivery.

(a) Tender of delivery requires that the seller put and hold conforming goods at the buyer's disposal and give any notification reasonably necessary for the buyer to take delivery. A tender of delivery includes the performance of any agreement to install or assemble the goods. Tender must be at a reasonable hour. A tender of goods must be kept available for the period reasonably necessary to enable the buyer to take possession or control of the goods. The buyer shall furnish facilities reasonably suited to receive the goods.

(b) If the seller is required or authorized to send the goods to the buyer but the agreement does not require delivery at a particular destination, tender requires that the seller deliver conforming goods to the carrier and comply with Section 2–603.

(c) If the agreement requires the seller to deliver at a particular destination, tender requires compliance with subsection (a) and, in an appropriate case, the tender of documents [of title] pursuant to subsections (d) and (e). The seller need not deliver at a particular destination unless required by a specific agreement or by the commercial understanding of the terms used by the parties. . . .

(e) If an agreement requires a seller to deliver a document [of title], the following rules apply:

(1) All required documents [of title] must be tendered in correct form, except as provided in this article with respect to bills of lading in a set.

(2) Tender through customary banking channels is sufficient, and dishonor of a draft or other demand for payment accompanying the documents constitutes nonacceptance or rejection.

§ 2–606. Effect of Seller's Tender; Delivery on Condition.

(a) Tender of delivery is a condition to a buyer's duty to accept and pay for the goods. Tender entitles the seller to acceptance of the goods and payment according to the agreement. The seller shall tender first but need not complete delivery until the buyer has tendered payment.

(b) Subject to Section 2–816, if payment is due and demanded on the delivery of goods or documents of title, a buyer's right against the seller to retain or dispose of them is conditional upon the buyer's making the payment due.

§ 2–607. Tender of Payment by Buyer; Payment by Check.

(a) Subject to Section 2–606(a), tender of payment by a buyer is a condition to the seller's duty to complete a delivery.

(b) Tender of payment by a buyer is sufficient if made by any means or in any manner current in the ordinary course of business unless the seller demands payment in money and gives any extension of time reasonably necessary to procure it.

§ 2–609. Buyer's Right to Inspect Goods.

(a) If goods are tendered, delivered or identified to a contract for sale, the buyer has a right before payment or acceptance to inspect them at any reasonable place and time and in any reasonable manner. If the seller is required or authorized to send the goods to the buyer, the inspection may be after their arrival.

(b) Expenses of inspection must be borne by the buyer.

(c) A buyer is not entitled to inspect the goods before payment of the price if the contract provides for:

(1) delivery "C.O.D.", "C.I.F.", or "C. & F." or delivery on terms which under applicable course of dealing, usage of trade, or course of performance are interpreted as precluding inspection before payment; or

(2) payment upon tender of required documents of title, unless payment is due only after the goods become available for inspection. . . .

§ 2–612. Risk of Loss.

(a) This section is subject to Section 2–506(b) and (c).

(b) Except as otherwise provided in subsection (c), risk of loss passes to the buyer regardless of the conformity of the goods to the contract as follows:

(1) Subject to this subsection, the risk of loss passes to a buyer upon receipt of the goods. If a buyer does not intend to take possession, risk of loss passes when the buyer receives control of the goods.

(2) If a contract requires or authorizes the seller to ship goods by carrier, the following rules apply:

(A) If the contract does not require delivery at a particular destination, the risk of loss passes to the buyer when the goods are delivered to the carrier as required by Sections 2–602 and 2–603, even if the shipment is under reservation.

(B) If the contract requires delivery at a particular destination and the goods arrive there in the possession of the carrier, the risk of loss passes to the buyer when goods are tendered in the manner required by Section 2–602. . . .

(c) A breach of contract by either party affects risk of loss only in the following cases:

(1) If the buyer rightfully and effectively rejects the goods or revokes acceptance of the goods, the seller has the risk of loss from the time when the rejection or revocation is effective.

(2) If the seller has tendered nonconforming goods, the risk of loss has passed to the buyer, and the goods are damaged or lost before the buyer effectively rejects or revokes acceptance, the seller has the risk of loss to the extent the nonconformity of the goods caused the damage or loss.

(3) If conforming goods are identified to the contract when the buyer repudiates or is otherwise in breach and the risk of loss has not otherwise passed to the buyer, the buyer has the risk of loss for those goods for a commercially reasonable time after the breach or repudiation.

PART 7

BREACH, REPUDIATION, AND EXCUSE

§ 2–701. Breach of Contract Generally; Substantial Impairment.

(a) Whether a party is in breach of contract is determined by the terms of the contract.

(b) A breach of contract occurs in the following circumstances, among others:

(1) A seller is in breach if it fails to deliver or to perform an obligation, makes a nonconforming tender of performance, or repudiates the contract.

(2) A buyer is in breach if it wrongfully rejects a tender of delivery, wrongfully revokes acceptance, repudiates the contract, or fails to make a required payment or to perform an obligation.

(c) To determine whether the value of an installment or the whole contract has been substantially impaired by a breach of contract under Section 2–708, 2–710, or 2–712, the court may consider whether:

(1) the extent to which the aggrieved party has been deprived of the benefit that it reasonably expected under the contract;

(2) cure of the breach is permitted and likely;

(3) adequate assurance of due performance has been given; and

(4) the party in breach acted in good faith.

(d) The cumulative effect of individual, insubstantial breaches of contract may substantially impair the value of the whole contract to the other party.

§ 2–702. Waiver of Breach; Particularization of Nonconformity.

(a) Except as provided in subsection (c), a party that knows that the other party's performance constitutes a breach of contract but accepts that performance and fails within a reasonable time to object is precluded from relying on the breach to cancel the contract. Except as otherwise provided in subsection (c), acceptance of that performance and failure to object do not preclude a claim for damages unless the party in breach has changed its position reasonably and in good faith in reliance on the aggrieved party's inaction.

(b) Failure to object to a nonconforming performance under subsection (a) does not foreclose objection to the same or similar breach of contract in future performances of like kind unless the party foreclosed expressly so states. A statement waiving future performance may be retracted by seasonable notification received by the other party that strict performance will be required unless the waiver has induced the other party to change its position reasonably and in good faith.

(c) A party is precluded from relying on a nonconforming performance as follows:

(1) Payment upon tender of documents [of title] made without reservation of rights waives the right to recover the payment for defects apparent on the face of the document [of title].

(2) A buyer's failure to state, in connection with a rejection under Section 2–703, a particular nonconformity that is ascertainable by reasonable inspection precludes reliance on the unstated defect to justify rejection or to establish a breach of contract if:

(A) the seller, upon a seasonable particularization, had a right to cure under Section 2–709 and [would] [could] have cured the [nonconformity] [breach]; or

(B) between merchants, the seller after rejection has made a request in a record for a full and final statement in a record of all nonconformities on which the buyer proposes to rely.

(3) A buyer's failure to state, in connection with a revocation of acceptance under Section 2–708, the nonconformity that justifies the revocation precludes the buyer from relying on the nonconformity to justify the revocation or to establish breach of contract if the seller had a right to cure the breach under Section 2–709 and [would] [could] have cured the breach.

§ 2–703. Buyer's Rights on Nonconforming Delivery; Rightful Rejection.

(a) Subject to Sections 2–603(b), 2–710, 2–809, and 2–810, if the goods or the tender of delivery fail in any respect to conform to the contract, a buyer may:

(1) reject the whole;

(2) accept the whole; or

(3) accept any commercial units and reject the rest.

(b) A rejection under subsection (a) is not effective unless the buyer notifies the seller within a reasonable time after [tender of delivery] [the nonconformity was or should have been discovered].

§ 2–704. Effect of Effective Rightful Rejection and Justifiable Revocation of Acceptance.

(a) Subject to Sections 2–705 and 2–829(b), after an effective rightful rejection or justifiable revocation of acceptance, a buyer that takes delivery shall hold the goods with reasonable care at the seller's disposition for a sufficient time to permit the seller to remove them. However, the buyer has no further obligation with regard to the goods.

(b) If a buyer uses the goods after an effective rightful rejection or justifiable revocation of acceptance, the following rules apply:

(1) Any use by the buyer which is inconsistent with the seller's ownership or with the buyer's claim of rejection or revocation of acceptance and is unreasonable under the circumstances is an acceptance if ratified by the seller.

(2) If use of the goods is reasonable under the circumstances and is not an acceptance, the buyer, upon returning or disposing of the goods, shall pay the seller the reasonable value of the use to the buyer. The value must be deducted from the sum of the price paid to the seller, if any, and any damages to which the buyer is otherwise entitled under this article.

(c) A buyer in possession that wrongfully but effectively rejects goods is subject to subsection (b)(1) and the duty of care in subsection (a).

§ 2–706. What Constitutes Acceptance of Goods.

(a) Goods are accepted when the buyer:

(1) states to the seller at any time that the goods are accepted;

(2) after a reasonable opportunity to inspect the goods, signifies to the seller that the goods conform or will be taken or retained in spite of their nonconformity;

(3) after a reasonable opportunity to inspect the goods, fails to make an effective rejection; or

(4) either before or after rejection or after revocation of acceptance, does any unreasonable act inconsistent with the seller's ownership or the buyer's claim of rejection or revocation of acceptance and that act is ratified by the seller as an acceptance.

(b) Acceptance of a part of a commercial unit is acceptance of the entire unit.

§ 2–707. Effect of Acceptance; Notice of Breach; Burden of Establishing Breach After Acceptance; Notice of Claim or Litigation to Person Answerable Over.

(a) A buyer shall pay the price in accordance with the contract for any goods accepted.

(b) Acceptance of goods by a buyer precludes rejection of the goods accepted but does not by itself impair any other remedy provided by this article for nonconformity.

(c) If a tender has been accepted, the following rules apply:

(1) The buyer, within a reasonable time after the buyer discovers or should have discovered a breach of contract, shall notify the party claimed against of the breach. However, a failure to give notice bars

the buyer from a remedy only to the extent that the party entitled to notice establishes that it was prejudiced by the failure.

(2) If a claim for infringement or the like is made against a buyer for which a seller is answerable over, the buyer shall notify the seller within a reasonable time after receiving notice of the litigation or be barred from any remedy over for liability established by the litigation.

(d) A buyer has the burden of establishing a breach of contract with respect to goods accepted. . . .

§ 2–708. Revocation of Acceptance.

(a) A buyer may revoke acceptance of a lot or commercial unit whose nonconformity substantially impairs its value to the buyer if the lot or unit was accepted:

(1) on the reasonable assumption that its nonconformity would be cured and it has not been seasonably cured; or

(2) without discovery of its nonconformity if acceptance was reasonably induced by the difficulty of discovery before acceptance or by the seller's assurances.

(b) To be effective, a buyer's acceptance must be revoked within a reasonable time after the buyer discovers or should have discovered the ground for it and before any substantial change in condition of the goods which is not caused by their own defects. The revocation is not effective until the buyer notifies the seller of it.

(c) A buyer that justifiably revokes acceptance has the same rights and duties under Sections 2–704 and 2–705 with regard to the goods as if they had been rejected.

§ 2–709. Cure.

(a) If a buyer effectively and rightfully rejects goods or a tender of delivery under Section 2–703 or justifiably revokes an acceptance under Section 2–708(a)(2) and the agreed time for performance has not expired, the seller, upon seasonable notice to the buyer and at its own expense, may cure any breach of contract by making a conforming tender of delivery within the agreed time and by compensating the buyer for all of the buyer's reasonable and necessary expenses caused by the nonconforming tender and subsequent cure.

(b) If a buyer effectively and rightfully rejects goods or a tender of delivery under Section 2–703 or justifiably revokes acceptance under Section 2–708(a)(2) and the agreed time for performance has expired, the seller, upon seasonable notice to the buyer and at its own expense, may cure the breach of contract by making a tender of conforming goods and by compensating the buyer for all of the buyer's reasonable and necessary expenses caused by the nonconforming tender and subsequent cure, if the cure is [appropriate and] timely under the circumstances and the buyer has no reasonable grounds to refuse the cure.

§ 2–710. Installment Contract: Breach.

(a) In this section, "installment contract" means a contract in which the terms require or the circumstances permit the delivery of goods in lots to be separately accepted, even if the agreement requires payment other than in installments or contains a term stating "Each delivery is a separate contract" or words of similar import.

(b) A buyer may reject any nonconforming installment of delivery of goods [or documents] in an installment contract if the nonconformity substantially impairs the value of that installment to the buyer [or if the nonconformity is a defect in the required documents]. [However, if a nonconforming tender by the seller is not a breach of the whole contract under subsection (c) and the seller gives adequate assurance of its cure, the buyer shall accept that installment.]

(c) If a nonconformity with respect to one or more installments in an installment contract is a substantial impairment of the value of the whole contract, there is a breach of the whole contract and the aggrieved party may cancel the contract. However, the power to cancel the contract for breach is waived, or a canceled contract is reinstated, if the aggrieved party accepts a nonconforming installment without seasonably giving notice of cancellation, brings an action with respect to only past installments, or demands performance as to future installments.

§ 2–711. Right to Adequate Assurance of Performance.

(a) A contract imposes an obligation on each party not to impair the other's expectation of receiving due performance. If reasonable grounds for insecurity arise with respect to the performance of either party, the other party may demand in a record adequate assurance of due performance and, until that assurance is received, if commercially reasonable, may suspend any performance for which the agreed return has not already been received.

(b) Between merchants, the reasonableness of grounds for insecurity and the adequacy of any assurance offered is determined according to commercial standards.

(c) Acceptance of improper delivery or payment does not prejudice an aggrieved party's right to demand adequate assurance of future performance.

(d) After receipt of a demand under subsection (a), failure to provide within a reasonable time, not exceeding 30 days, assurance of due performance which is adequate under the circumstances of the particular case is a repudiation of the contract under Section 2–712(a).

§ 2–712. Anticipatory Repudiation.

(a) If either party to a contract repudiates a performance not yet due and the loss of performance will substantially impair the value of the contract to the other party, the aggrieved party may:

(1) await performance by the repudiating party for a commercially reasonable time or resort to any remedy for breach of contract, even if

it has urged the repudiating party to retract the repudiation or has notified the repudiating party that it would await the agreed performance; and

(2) in either case, suspend its own performance or, if a seller, proceed in accordance with Section 2–817.

(b) Repudiation includes language that one party will not or cannot make a performance still due under the contract or voluntary affirmative conduct that reasonably appears to the other party to make a future performance impossible.

§ 2–713. Retraction of Anticipatory Repudiation.

(a) A repudiating party may retract a repudiation until its next performance is due unless the aggrieved party, after the repudiation, has canceled the contract, materially changed its position, or otherwise indicated that the repudiation is considered to be final.

(b) A retraction may be by any method that clearly indicates to the aggrieved party that the repudiating party intends to perform the contract. However, a retraction must contain any assurance demanded under Section 2–711.

(c) Retraction reinstates a repudiating party's rights under the contract with due excuse and allowance to the aggrieved party for any delay caused by the repudiation.

§ 2–714. Casualty to Identified Goods.

If the parties to a contract assume the continued existence and eventual delivery to the buyer of goods identified when the contract is made and the goods suffer casualty without the fault of either party before the risk of loss passes to the buyer and no commercially reasonable substitute is available, the following rules apply:

(1) The seller shall seasonably notify the buyer of the nature and extent of the loss.

(2) If the loss is total, the contract is avoided [terminated].

(3) If the loss is partial or the goods no longer conform to the contract, the buyer may nevertheless demand inspection and may treat the contract as avoided or accept the goods with due allowance from the price for the nonconformity but without further right against the seller.

§ 2–715. Substituted Performance.

(a) If, without the fault of either party, agreed berthing, loading, or unloading facilities or an agreed type of carrier becomes unavailable, or an agreed manner of delivery otherwise becomes commercially impracticable, an aggrieved party may claim excuse under Section 2–716 unless a commercially reasonable substitute is available. In that case, reasonable substitute performance must be tendered and accepted.

(b) If an agreed means or manner of payment fails because of domestic or foreign governmental regulation, the seller may withhold or stop delivery until the buyer provides a means or manner of payment which is commercially a substantial equivalent. If delivery has already been made, payment by the means or in the manner provided by the regulation discharges the buyer's obligation unless the regulation is discriminatory, oppressive, or predatory.

§ 2–716. Excuse by Failure of Presupposed Conditions.

(a) Subject to Section 2–715 and subsection (b), delay in performance or nonperformance by the seller is not a breach of contract if the seller's performance as agreed has been made impracticable by:

(1) the occurrence of a contingency whose nonoccurrence was a basic assumption on which the contract was made; or

(2) compliance in good faith with any applicable foreign or domestic governmental regulation, statute, or order, whether or not it later proves to be invalid.

(b) A party claiming excuse under subsection (a) shall seasonably notify the other party that there will be delay or nonperformance. If the claimed excuse affects only a part of the seller's capacity to perform, the seller shall also allocate production and deliveries among its customers in a manner that is fair and reasonable and notify the buyer of the estimated quota made available. In allocating production and deliveries, the seller may include regular customers not then under contract as well as its own requirements for further manufacture.

§ 2–717. Procedure on Notification Claiming Excuse.

(a) A party that receives notification of a material or indefinite delay in performance or an allocation permitted under Section 2–714 or 2–716 as to any delivery concerned, or if there is a breach of the whole contract under Section 2–710(c), then as to the whole, by notification in a record, may:

(1) terminate and thereby discharge any unexecuted portion of the contract; or

(2) modify the contract by agreeing to take the available allocation in substitution under Section 2–716 [or by accepting the goods with due allowance as provided in Section 2–714].

(b) If, after receipt of notification under Section 2–714 or 2–716, a party fails to terminate or modify the contract within a reasonable time not exceeding 30 days, the contract lapses [is terminated] with respect to any performance affected.

(c) This section may be varied by agreement only to the extent that the parties have assumed a different obligation under Sections 2–714 and 2–716.

PART 8

REMEDIES

[A. IN GENERAL]

§ 2–801. Subject to General Limitations.

The remedies of the seller, buyer, and other protected persons under this article are subject to the general limitations and principles stated in Sections 2–801 through 2–814.

§ 2–802. Breach of Contract; Procedures.

If a party is in breach of a contract, the party seeking enforcement:

(1) has the rights and remedies in this article and, except as limited by this part, in the agreement;

(2) may reduce its claim to judgment or otherwise enforce the contract by any available administrative or judicial procedure, or the like, including arbitration if agreed to by the parties; and

(3) may enforce the rights granted by and remedies available under other law.

§ 2–803. Remedies in General.

(a) In accordance with Section 1–106, the remedies provided in this article must be liberally administered with the purpose of placing the aggrieved party in as good a position as if the other party had fully performed.

(b) Unless the contract provides for liquidated damages under Section 2–809 or a limited remedy enforceable under Section 2–810, an aggrieved party may not recover that part of a loss resulting from a breach of contract that could have been avoided by reasonable measures under the circumstances. The burden of establishing a failure to take reasonable measures under the circumstances is on the party in breach.

(c) The rights granted by and remedies available under this article are cumulative, but a party may not recover more than once for the same injury. [Unless the contract provides for liquidated damages or a limited remedy enforceable under Section 2–809 or 2–810, a court may deny or limit a remedy if, under the circumstances, it would put the aggrieved party in a substantially better position than if the party in breach had fully performed.]

(d) This article does not impair a remedy for breach of any obligation or promise collateral or ancillary to a contract for sale.

§ 2–804. Measurement of Damages in General.

If there is a breach of contract, the aggrieved party may recover compensation for the loss resulting in the ordinary course from the breach as determined under Sections 2–815 through 2–829 or as determined in any reasonable manner, together with incidental damages and consequential damages, less expenses and costs avoided as a result of the breach.

§ 2–805. Incidental Damages.

Incidental damages resulting from breach of contract include compensation for any commercially reasonable charges, expenses, or commissions incurred with respect to:

(1) inspection, receipt, transportation, care, and custody of identified goods which are the subject of the breached contract;

(2) stopping delivery or shipment;

(3) effecting cover, return, or resale of the goods;

(4) reasonable efforts otherwise to minimize or avoid the consequences of breach; and

(5) otherwise dealing with the goods or effectuating other remedies.

§ 2–806. Consequential Damages.

(a) Consequential damages resulting from a breach of contract include compensation for:

(1) any loss, including loss to property other than the goods sold, the party in breach at the time of contracting had reason to know would probably result from the aggrieved party's general or particular requirements and needs and which could not have been avoided by reasonable measures under the circumstances; and

(2) injury to person proximately resulting from any breach of warranty.

(b) The aggrieved party may not recover any consequential damages pursuant to subsection (a)(1) that result in disproportionate compensation to the aggrieved party. The breaching party has the burden of establishing that consequential damages under subsection (a)(1) result in disproportionate compensation.

§ 2–807. Specific Performance.

(a) A court may enter a decree for specific performance if the parties have expressly agreed to that remedy or the goods or the agreed performance of the party in breach of contract are unique or in other proper circumstances. Even if the parties expressly agree to specific performance, a court shall not enter a decree for specific performance where the breaching party's sole remaining contractual obligation is the payment of money.

(b) A decree for specific performance may contain terms and conditions as to payment of the price or damages or other relief the court considers just.

§ 2–808. Cancellation: Effect.

(a) An aggrieved party may cancel a contract if there is a breach under Section 2–701, or in the case of an installment contract, a breach of the whole contract under Section 2–710(c), unless there is a waiver of the breach under Section 2–702 or a right to cure the breach under Section 2–709.

(b) Cancellation is not effective until the canceling party notifies the party in breach of the cancellation.

(c) Except as otherwise provided in subsection (d), upon cancellation, all obligations that are still executory on both sides are discharged.

(d) The obligations surviving cancellation include:

(1) a right based on a previous breach or performance of a contract;

(2) any term limiting disclosure of information;

(3) an obligation to return or dispose of goods;

(4) a choice of law forum;

(5) an obligation to arbitrate or otherwise resolve disputes through alternative dispute resolution procedures;

(6) a term limiting the time for commencing an action or for providing notice;

(7) a remedy for breach of the whole contract or any unperformed balance; and

(8) other rights, remedies, or limitations if in the circumstances such survival is necessary to achieve the purposes of the parties.

(e) Unless a contrary intention clearly appears, language of cancellation, rescission, or avoidance of the contract or similar language is not a renunciation or discharge of any claim in damages for an antecedent breach of contract.

§ 2–809. Liquidation of Damages; Deposits.

(a) Damages for breach of contract may be liquidated [in the contract] but only in an amount that is reasonable in the light of the difficulties of proof of loss in the event of breach and either the actual loss or the then anticipated loss caused by the breach. If a term liquidating damages is unenforceable under this subsection, the aggrieved party may pursue the remedies provided in this article.

(b) If a seller justifiably withholds or stops performance because of the buyer's breach of contract or insolvency, the buyer is entitled to restitution of the amount by which the sum of payments exceeds the amount to which the seller is entitled under a term liquidating damages in accordance with subsection (a).

(c) A buyer's right to restitution under subsection (b) is subject to offset to the extent that the seller establishes a right to recover damages under the provisions of this article other than subsection (a) and the amount or value of any benefits received by the buyer directly or indirectly by reason of the contract.

(d) If a buyer has received payment in goods, their reasonable value or the proceeds of their resale are payments for the purposes of subsection (b).

§ 2–810. Contractual Modification of Remedy.

(a) Subject to Section 2–809, the following rules apply:

(1) An agreement may add to, limit, or substitute for the remedies available under this article, such as by limiting or altering the measure of damages recoverable for breach of contract or limiting the buyer's remedies to return of the goods and repayment by the seller of the price or to repair and replacement of nonconforming goods or parts by the seller.

(2) An agreed remedy under paragraph (1) may not be applied to deprive the aggrieved party of a minimum adequate remedy under the circumstances.

(3) Resort to an agreed remedy under paragraph (1) is optional. However, if the parties expressly agree that the agreed remedy is exclusive, it is the sole remedy.

(b) Subject to subsection (a)(2), if, because of a breach of contract or other circumstances, an exclusive, agreed remedy fails substantially to achieve the intended purposes of the parties, the following rules apply:

(1) In a contract other than a consumer contract, the aggrieved party may pursue all remedies available under this article. However, an agreement expressly providing that incidental or consequential damages, including those resulting from the failure to provide the limited remedy, are excluded is enforceable to the extent permitted under subsection (c).

(2) In a consumer contract, an aggrieved party may reject the goods or revoke acceptance and, to the extent of the failure, may pursue all remedies available under this article including the right to recover consequential or incidental damages, despite any term purporting to exclude or limit such remedies.

(c) Subject to subsection (b), consequential damages and incidental damages may be limited or excluded by agreement unless the limitation or exclusion is unconscionable. Limitation of consequential damages for injury to the person in the case of a consumer contract is presumed to be unconscionable.

§ 2–811. Remedies for Misrepresentation or Fraud.

Remedies for material misrepresentation or fraud include all remedies available under this article for nonfraudulent breach of contract. Rescission or a claim for rescission of a contract for sale and rejection or return of the goods do not bar a claim for damages or other consistent remedy.

§ 2–812. Proof of Market Price.

(a) If evidence of a price prevailing at a time or place described in this article is not readily available, the following rules apply:

(1) The price prevailing within any reasonable time before or after the time described may be used.

(2) The price prevailing at any other place that in commercial judgment or usage of trade is a reasonable substitute may be used, making proper allowance for any cost of transporting the goods to or from the other place.

(3) Evidence of a relevant price prevailing at another time or place offered by one party is not admissible unless the party has given the other party notice that the court finds sufficient to prevent unfair surprise.

(b) If the prevailing price or value of goods regularly bought and sold in any established commodity market is in dispute, reports in official publications or trade journals or in newspapers, periodicals, or other means of communication in general circulation and published as the reports of that market are admissible in evidence. The circumstances of the preparation of such a report may affect the weight of the evidence but not its admissibility.

§ 2–814. Statute of Limitations.

(a) An action for breach of a contract under this article must be commenced within the later of four years after the right of action has accrued or one year after the breach was or should have been discovered, but no longer than five years after the right of action accrued. Except in a consumer contract or an action for indemnity, the original agreement may reduce the period of limitation to not less than one year.

(b) Except as otherwise provided in subsection (c) and (d) and Sections 2–402(e) and 2–404(e), a right of action for breach of contract accrues when the breach occurs, even if the aggrieved party did not have knowledge of the breach. For purposes of this section, a breach by repudiation occurs when the aggrieved party learns of the repudiation.

(c) If a breach of warranty occurs, the following rules apply:

(1) Subject to paragraph (2), a right of action for breach of warranty accrues when the seller has completed tender of delivery of the nonconforming goods.

(2) If a warranty expressly extends to performance of the goods after delivery, a right of action accrues when the buyer discovers or should have discovered the breach.

(d) A right of action for indemnity accrues when the act or omission on which the claim for indemnity is based is or should have been discovered by the indemnified party.

(e) If an action for breach of contract is commenced within the applicable time limitation is terminated but a remedy by another action for the same breach of contract is available, the other action may be commenced after the expiration of the time limitation and within six months after the termination of the first action unless the termination resulted from voluntary discontinuance or from dismissal for failure to prosecute.

(f) This section does not alter the law on tolling of a statute of limitations and does not apply to a right of action that accrued before the effective date of this article.

[B.   SELLER'S REMEDIES]

§ 2–815. Seller's Remedies in General.

If a buyer breaches the contract under Section 2–701 or 2–710(c) becomes insolvent, the seller may:

(1) withhold delivery of the goods under Section 2–816(a) or 2–818(a);

(2) stop delivery of the goods under Section 2–818(b);

(3) proceed with respect to goods still unidentified to the contract or unfinished under Section 2–817;

(4) reclaim the goods under Section 2–816(b);

(5) obtain specific performance under Section 2–807 or recover the price under Section 2–822;

(6) resell the goods and recover damages under Section 2–819;

(7) recover damages for repudiation or nonacceptance under Section 2–821;

(8) recover incidental and consequential damages under Sections 2–805 and 2–806;

(9) cancel the contract under Section 2–808;

(10) recover liquidated damages under Section 2–809;

(11) enforce limited remedies under Section 2–810; or

(12) recover damages under Section 2–804.

§ 2–816. Seller's Right to Withhold Delivery of Goods or to Reclaim Goods After Delivery to Buyer.

(a) If a buyer is in breach of contract under Section 2–701, the seller may withhold delivery of the goods directly affected. If the breach is of the whole contract, Section 2–710(c), the seller may withhold delivery of any undelivered balance.

(b) Under this article, a seller may reclaim goods delivered to a buyer under a contract for sale only in the following circumstances:

(1) A seller that discovers that the buyer has received goods on credit while insolvent may reclaim the goods upon a demand made in a record within 10 days after receipt of the goods or, if a bankruptcy case in which the buyer is the debtor is commenced during the 10 day period, such demand must be made within 20 days after receipt of the goods. If the buyer made a material misrepresentation of a credit

107

condition in a record to the reclaiming seller or to a credit reporting agency or the like less than 90 days before delivery, the demand is timely if made within a reasonable time after delivery.

(2) If payment is due and demanded on delivery to the buyer, the seller may reclaim the goods delivered upon a demand made within a reasonable time after the seller discovers or should have discovered that payment was not made.

(c) Reclamation is subject to the rights under this article of a buyer in ordinary course of business or other good-faith purchaser for value that arise before the seller takes possession under a timely demand for reclamation. Successful reclamation of the goods under subsection (b)(1) precludes all other remedies with respect to them.

§ 2–817. Seller's Right to Identify Goods to Contract Despite Breach or to Salvage Unfinished Goods.

(a) An aggrieved seller may:

(1) identify to the contract conforming goods not already identified if they are in the seller's possession or control at the time the seller learned of the breach of contract; and

(2) resell goods that are shown to have been intended for the particular contract, even if they are unfinished.

(b) If goods are unfinished at the time of breach of contract, an aggrieved seller, in the exercise of reasonable commercial judgment to minimize loss and for the purpose of effective realization, may complete the manufacture and wholly identify the goods to the contract, cease manufacture and resell for scrap or salvage value, or proceed in any other reasonable manner.

§ 2–818. Seller's Refusal to Deliver Because of Buyer's Insolvency; Stoppage in Transit or Otherwise.

(a) A seller that discovers that the buyer is insolvent may refuse to make delivery except for cash, including payment for all goods previously delivered under the contract.

(b) Subject to subsection (d), a seller may stop delivery of goods in the possession of a carrier or other bailee if the buyer is insolvent or repudiates or fails to make a payment due before delivery or if, for any other reason, the seller has a right to withhold or reclaim the goods.

(c) As against a buyer under subsection (b), the seller may stop delivery until:

(1) receipt of the goods by the buyer;

(2) acknowledgment to the buyer by any bailee of the goods, other than a carrier, or by a carrier by reshipment or as warehouseman, that the bailee holds the goods for the buyer; or

(3) negotiation to the buyer of any negotiable document of title covering the goods. . . .

§ 2–819. Seller's Resale.

(a) If a buyer has breached a contract and the goods concerned are in the seller's possession or control, the seller may resell them or the undelivered balance. If the resale is made in good faith, within a commercially reasonable time, and in a commercially reasonable manner, the seller may recover the contract price less the resale price together with any consequential and incidental damages, less expenses avoided as a result of the breach.

(b) A resale:

(1) may be at a public auction or private sale including sale by one or more contracts to sell or by identification to an existing contract of the seller;

(2) may be as a unit or in parcels and at any time and place and on any terms, but every aspect of the sale, including the method, manner, time, place, and terms, must be commercially reasonable; and

(3) must be reasonably identified as referring to the breached contract, but the goods need not be in existence or have been identified to the contract before the breach.

(c) If the resale is at a public auction, the following rules apply:

(1) Only identified goods may be sold unless there is a recognized market for the public sale of futures in goods of the kind.

(2) The resale must be made at a usual place or market for public sale if one is reasonably available. Except in the case of goods that are perishable or which threaten to decline in value speedily, the seller shall give the buyer reasonable notice of the time and place of the resale.

(3) If the goods are not to be within the view of persons attending the sale, the notification of sale must state the place where the goods are located and provide for their reasonable inspection by prospective bidders.

(4) The seller may buy the goods.

(d) A good-faith purchaser at a resale takes the goods free of any rights of the original buyer, even if the seller fails to comply with this section.

(e) A seller is not accountable to the buyer for any profit made on a resale. However, a person in the position of a seller or a buyer which has rightfully rejected or justifiably revoked acceptance shall account for any excess over the amount of the claim secured by the security interest as provided in Section 2–823(b).

§ 2–821. Seller's Damages for Nonacceptance, Failure to Pay, or Repudiation.

(a) If a buyer breaches a contract, the seller may recover damages based upon market price, together with any incidental and consequential damages, less expenses avoided as a result of the breach, as follows:

109

(1) Except as provided in subsection (2), the measure of damages is the contract price less the market price of comparable goods at the time and place for tender.

(2) In the case of a repudiation governed by Section 2–712, the measure of damages is the contract price less the market price of comparable goods at the place for tender and at the time when a commercially reasonable period after the seller learned of the repudiation has expired. The commercially reasonable time includes the time for awaiting a retraction under Section 2–712 and the time needed to obtain substitute performance.

(b) A seller may recover damages measured by other than the market price, together with incidental and consequential damages, including:

(1) lost profits, including reasonable overhead, resulting from the breach of contract determined in any reasonable manner; and

(2) reasonable expenditures made in preparing for or performing the contract if, after the breach, the seller is unable to obtain reimbursement by salvage, resale, or other reasonable measures.

§ 2–822. Action for Price.

(a) If a buyer fails to pay the price as it becomes due, the seller may recover, together with any incidental and consequential damages, the price of:

(1) goods accepted;

(2) conforming goods lost or damaged after risk of their loss has passed to the buyer, but, if the seller has retained or regained control of the goods, the loss or damage must occur within a commercially reasonable time after the risk of loss has passed to the buyer; and

(3) goods identified to the contract, if the seller is unable after a reasonable effort to resell them at a reasonable price or the circumstances reasonably indicate that this effort would be unavailing.

(b) A seller that remains in control of the goods and sues for the price shall hold for the buyer any goods identified to the contract. If the seller is entitled to the price and resale becomes possible, the seller may resell the goods under Section 2–819 at any time before the collection of the judgment. The net proceeds of the resale must be credited to the buyer. Payment of the judgment entitles the buyer to any goods not resold.

(c) If a buyer has breached the contract, a seller that has sued for but is held not entitled to the price under this section may still be awarded damages for nonacceptance under Section 2–821.

[C. BUYER'S REMEDIES]

§ 2–823. Buyer's Remedies in General; Buyer's Security Interest in Rejected Goods.

If a seller is in breach of the contract under Section 2–701, or in breach of the whole contract under Section 2–710(c), the aggrieved buyer may:

(1) recover the price paid under Section 2–829(a) or deduct damages from price unpaid under Section 2–828;

(2) cancel the contract under Section 2–808;

(3) cover and obtain damages under Section 2–825;

(4) recover damages for nondelivery or repudiation under Section 2–826;

(5) recover damages for breach with regard to accepted goods under Section 2–827.

(6) recover identified goods under Section 2–824;

(7) obtain specific performance under Section 2–807;

(8) enforce a security interest under Section 2–829(b);

(9) recover incidental and consequential damages under Sections 2–805 and 2–806;

(10) recover liquidated damages under Section 2–809;

(11) enforce limited remedies under Section 2–810; or

(12) recover damages under Section 2–804.

§ 2–824. Prepaying Buyer's Right to Goods; Replevin.

(a) A buyer that pays all or a part of the price of goods identified to the contract, whether or not they have been shipped, on making and keeping good a tender of full performance, has a right to recover them from the seller if the seller repudiates or fails to deliver as required by the contract.

(b) A buyer may recover from the seller by replevin, detinue, sequestration, claim and delivery, or the like, goods identified to a contract if, after reasonable efforts, the buyer is unable to effect cover for the goods or the circumstances indicate that an effort to obtain cover would be unavailing or if the goods have been shipped under reservation and satisfaction of the security interest in them has been made or tendered.

(c) If the requirements of subsection (a) or (b) are satisfied, the buyer's right vests upon identification of the goods to the contract for sale even if the seller has not then repudiated the contract or failed to deliver as required by the contract.

§ 2–825. Cover; Buyer's Purchase of Substitute Goods.

(a) If a seller breaches a contract, the buyer may cover by making in good faith and without unreasonable delay any reasonable purchase of, contract to purchase, or arrangement to procure comparable goods to substitute for those due from the seller.

(b) A buyer that covers in the manner required by subsection (a) may recover damages measured by the cost of covering less the contract price, together with any incidental or consequential damages, less expenses avoided as a result of the seller's breach.

(c) A buyer that fails to cover in a manner required under subsection (a) is not barred from any other available remedy.

§ 2–826. Buyer's Damages for Nondelivery or Repudiation.

(a) If a seller breaches a contract, the buyer may recover damages based on market price, together with any incidental and consequential damages, less expenses avoided in consequence of the seller's breach, as follows:

(1) Except as provided in subsection (2), the measure of damages is the market price for comparable goods at the time of the breach or when the buyer learned of the breach, whichever is later, less the contract price.

(2) In the case of a repudiation governed by Section 2–712, the measure of damages is the market price of comparable goods at the time when a commercially reasonable period after the buyer learned of the breach has expired less the contract price. The commercially reasonable time includes the time for awaiting a retraction under Section 2–712 and the time needed to obtain substitute performance.

(b) Market price is determined at the place for tender. However, in cases of rejection after arrival or revocation of acceptance, it is determined at the place of arrival.

§ 2–827. Buyer's Damages for Breach Regarding Accepted Goods.

(a) A buyer that has accepted goods and not justifiably revoked acceptance and has given notice pursuant to Section 2–707(c)(1) may recover as damages for any nonconforming tender the loss resulting in the ordinary course of events from the seller's breach as determined in any reasonable manner.

(b) A measure of damages for breach of a warranty of quality is the value of the goods as warranted less the value of the goods accepted at the time and place of acceptance [unless special circumstances show proximate damages of a different amount].

(c) A buyer may recover incidental and consequential damages.

§ 2–828. Deduction of Damages From Price.

A buyer, on so notifying a seller, may deduct all or any part of the damages resulting from any breach from any part of the contract price still owed under the same contract.

§ 2–829. Recovery of Price; Buyer's Security Interest in Rejected Goods.

(a) If the seller has breached the contract, the buyer may recover any payments made on the price of goods that are not accepted.

(b) On rightful rejection or justifiable revocation of acceptance, a buyer has a security interest in goods in the buyer's possession or control for any payments made on their price and any expenses reasonably incurred in their inspection, receipt, transportation, care, and custody. The buyer may hold the goods and resell them in the manner provided for an aggrieved seller under Section 2–819, except that the buyer shall give the seller reasonable notice of the intended resale and must account to the seller for any excess of the proceeds of resale over the amount of the security interest created in this subsection.